Reading Intervention Behind School Walls

Why Your Child Continues To Struggle

By Faith Borkowsky, M.S.
Certified Dyslexia Practitioner

DEDICATION

This book is dedicated to the families of those courageous children who go to school each and every day believing they can learn when learning does not come easily. I am in awe of your commitment and dedication, and I am honored to work with you.

CONTENTS

ACKNOWLEDGMENTS

To my wonderful husband, Mitch, for supporting me in every endeavor. Thank you, thank you, thank you for being my line editor, copy editor, page formatter, and the best dancing partner I could ever ask for. You are, and always will be, my best friend.

To my children, Matt and Ariel, for encouraging me to write this book, gifting me a journal and pen, and believing that I can. Forever and always in my heart, you are both my inspiration.

To my parents. For everything. I love you, always.

INTRODUCTION

A CHILD AND FAMILY IN CRISIS

Robert's emotional state was suffering. He was so distraught about not being able to function in school and felt so humiliated about his inability to read, he actually contemplated suicide. It was at that point that his mother pulled him out of school and made the difficult and terrifying decision to homeschool him. She worried if he would have a social life. She worried whether the family could afford to lose a paycheck if she gave up her job. And she worried whether she had the skills to teach her own son to read. Robert's siblings were not homeschooled, and this would be a leap of faith to save her youngest child. Robert was a fourth grader when this journey began.

I was introduced to this desperate family through my husband's coworker after the decision to homeschool was finalized. Robert was a handsome, charming boy who was raised in a loving family. If you looked at him, he appeared confident and happy. Well, appearances are deceiving. I evaluated Robert and found his skills to be at a beginner first grade level. He had been pulled out for reading services in school for years and had made virtually no progress. He had poor phonemic awareness and could not blend sounds together to read a word. He had no understanding of how letter combinations map to the sounds in the English language, and he guessed his way through the assessment. No surprise that his writing and spelling were equally poor. Robert's mother was overwhelmed not knowing where to begin. I told her that I could help both of them, but she would need to be very involved in the process because the work required was intensive. I could not have asked for a more able parent to coach her child.

I began working with Robert in a non-traditional way. Rather than start

1

with reading, I began working on trust and stress reduction techniques to break his defeatist attitude. After all, nobody else had helped him yet, so why should I be any different? Children are quite intuitive and can sense when someone is being disingenuous. Luckily, Robert's mother was receptive and allowed me to begin to build a relationship with her son. With twice weekly sessions using a scientifically, research-based multisensory program, Robert began reading for the first time. It was a slow, steady climb, and he continued to struggle due to his learning disabilities. But Robert realized that he could improve, and he learned to recognize strategies that worked for him. Robert returned to his school district the following year having improved tremendously, and both he and his mother were in a better position to advocate for themselves.

So where did the system fail Robert?

PART I: THE BUTTERFLY EFFECT

ONE SMALL CHANGE

When one small change leads to drastic results it is known as the Butterfly Effect. Believe it or not, the flap of a butterfly's wing in Brazil spurred catastrophic events leading to a tornado in Texas. Forecasting the future is not an exact science. Meteorologists try their best to track weather patterns and make predictions, but it is hard to predict all the factors, big and small, that lead to the exact moment a storm will strike.

This reminds me of how one small change in American education led to out-of-control illiteracy rates more than any other change - the marginalization of phonics in the kindergarten through third grade classrooms. One might argue, and I would agree, that poverty, lack of books in the home, parents' level of education, stress, and a host of other factors combine to affect literacy. Those factors, however, are difficult to overcome, and billions and billions of dollars have been spent on social programs to level the playing field. Innumerable state and federal initiatives have tried to solve the problems, yet we still have dismal results. 32 million adults in the U.S. can't read, 21 percent of adults read below a 5th grade level, 19 percent of high school "graduates" are illiterate, and over 70 percent of prison inmates cannot read above a fourth grade level. This was not always the case. America used to be one of the most literate countries in the world, despite poverty, crime, unsafe neighborhoods, and other adverse conditions.

If we look at the one "small" change that is fundamentally at the core of the problem, we can see that the teaching philosophy espoused today is not aligned with how all children, whether affluent or disadvantaged, can become successful readers. Rather than assume children will learn to read through osmosis, strong, bottom-up principles are needed that begin with teaching how sounds in our language are represented by letters, followed by learning left-to-right sequences of letters that make up words, and leading to an understanding of organized words that make up sentences and represent coherent thought.

Children should not be left to "discover" how words work. For a while, I was optimistic that the tide was turning with scientific research that supported early instruction in systematic phonics. Unfortunately, what we have now is a mixed-methods approach that waters down the intensity needed to make a difference. When children are encouraged to look at context and "search for meaning" before they have mastered letter and sound correspondence, we create confusion and failure. The flap of this butterfly's wing produced a functionally illiterate society, and there is no end to the damage that continues to be inflicted on emergent readers and writers.

In my thirty years as an educator, the stories are numerous, both heartwarming and heartbreaking. It is my hope that this book will raise questions and serve as a resource for those who are left confused, frustrated, and disgusted by the mixed messages given by politicians, school district officials, elite universities, and publishing companies. My goal is to educate parents and caregivers on issues related to literacy; however, more importantly, I would like to provide you with information to allow you to discern fact from fiction. Despite decades of effort by government officials and education gurus to raise standards, we are no better off today getting children to read well by the end of third grade. Why can't we find an answer?

Incorrect diagnoses and remediation that is "too little, too late" are just some of the reasons for the large number of people who cannot read or choose not to read in this country. When combined with "one-size-fits-all" teaching in classrooms, the proliferation of special interest groups promoting and perpetuating ineffective teaching methods, and children being pulled out for Academic Intervention Services (AIS) that do not address the fundamental issues, it is no wonder so many children continue to struggle learning to read. How do I know this? Having been a classroom teacher, reading and learning specialist, mentor, and administrator, I have witnessed firsthand this unfortunate reality.

When I began teaching in 1986, I was 21 years old and had just graduated from Brooklyn College. I dual majored in elementary education and special education, hoping to have been given the tools to work with all children, including those with special needs. In all my coursework, phonics was hardly mentioned. These were the years when a whole language philosophy infiltrated universities and schools across the country. Phonics was considered old-fashioned, not something that needed to be taught explicitly since it was assumed children would just pick it up. We were told that if we give children a love of books and surround them with words, they would be able to become avid readers. Just like that. And we were all anxious to get into classrooms and give children this gift. But I didn't see that happening during my student teaching experiences. We were placed in classrooms, both mainstream and special education, and I did not see most children learning to read easily. As a matter of fact, the children I saw could not spell, could not write, and could barely read at all. I figured that it must just be my student-teacher placements, and I trusted that when I had my own classroom, things would be different.

My first teaching experience was a third grade classroom in the Mill Basin section of Brooklyn, N.Y., an upper middle class area, where poverty was not a factor. As a new teacher, I did not have advanced readers in my class, but I was ambitious and excited to begin working my magic. The Open Court basal reader, a successful phonics-heavy program that was used for many years was being discarded and all vestiges of it removed from the school, including every letter/sound card hanging on the walls. Yippee! I thought. It was a new generation, and I was coming in at the right time. The seasoned teachers, however, did not feel the same way, and many of them hid their sound cards in their rooms and kept a few of the old readers stashed in their closets. They were going to continue to do what they knew worked, even if it was done behind closed doors. Well, my classroom would be different. I was ready to surround my room with books and words, and my children would learn to read through osmosis. I did everything I had learned in my college courses and more. I spent tons of money buying my own materials and purchasing books through my Scholastic book orders. I created a "literacy-rich environment."

I did not see what I was hoping to see. My third graders still spelled words using inventive spelling, wrote essays without proper punctuation, and guessed their way through books. They were not figuring it out, even with the most child-friendly library at their fingertips. I asked the two resource room teachers for suggestions. Both were close to thirty years old, young and bright, and had more experience than I had. They basically told me the same thing I learned in my college coursework. They gave me some "word-solving" strategies, but nothing concrete. After my first year of teaching, I decided to enroll in a Master's degree program in Reading. I was not satisfied that I had become a teacher with two certifications but could not help the struggling students in my class. Now, I would surely be able to help children.

My coursework consisted of children's and adolescent literature, author studies, journal writing, diagnostics, and finally, remediation. Yet, there was no mention of the Orton-Gillingham approach, a language-based, multisensory, structured, sequential method of teaching all 44 individual sounds with their possible letter combinations. All remediation was through whole language; we were taught to "analyze miscues" while children were reading to see the types of errors they made and instruct them to look at the shape, size, and beginning of the word. "Get your mouth ready." "What sound is at the beginning?" "Look at the picture." "Does your word make sense?" "Check your understanding," were some of the catch phrases I learned. There was no direct, explicit instruction of how letters are matched to sounds all through the word. At the completion of my degree, I knew more about genre, text structure, picture books, and comprehension strategies, but I did not have a deep understanding of the alphabetic code. I eventually became a reading teacher in the same district, using all the diagnostics and strategies that I learned, and I was able to help some children whose reading problems were not profound.

It was not until the late nineties, having moved to Long Island and teaching in Nassau County, that I read a book that would change the course of my life. The book literally fell off the shelf at Book Review in Huntington Village while I was just perusing the education section. The book was entitled, *Why Our Children Can't Read and What We Can Do About It: A Scientific Revolution in Reading,* by cognitive psychologist Diane McGuinness, published in 1999. It had exactly the information I was seeking. I began learning everything I could about a phonics-based approach, traveling to Washington D.C. for training in a program called Phono-Graphix and spending one summer in an Orton-Gillingham course through the International Dyslexia Association. The more I learned, the more I realized how many children did not have to struggle if they were taught with a phonics-based approach from the start and were given enough practice opportunities to really learn how to read, write, and spell. The schools, including the one at which I was teaching, were slow to change, and the "Reading Wars" began heating up.

It was a time of great controversy between whole language advocates and those believing in the science of reading. I could never go back to teaching the same way after discovering what really worked. I continued my learning and became knowledgeable in a number of structured language programs, all multisensory, and all with proven results. Most educators continued to use guided reading methods, and continued to espouse a whole language philosophy, but I couldn't follow along anymore. I began moving in a different direction, leaving the public school system to start my own reading and writing clinic. Eventually I became a regional reading coach for a federally funded literacy grant. In that position I worked with teachers and administrators across Long Island, offering embedded professional development in interventions for struggling readers. Over many years of being in school buildings and in numerous classrooms, I was able to observe different programs and strategies. Through observation and first-hand experience working with children, I was in an ideal position to gauge which programs were consistently beneficial for the majority of children, including those with special needs, English language learners, or just children needing a more direct, explicit approach. The programs that were the best were the ones that were used least. Why?

THE EMPEROR'S NEW CLOTHES

I am sure most of you are familiar with the Hans Christian Andersen's tale, "The Emperor's New Clothes. Here's a quick summary: Once upon a time, there was an emperor who loved fashion. He changed his clothes often and lovingly looked at himself whenever he had the chance. Two con artists came up with a scheme; they told the emperor that they were tailors and had a special material that is so light, only ignorant people would think it is invisible. The emperor, a real fashion-forward kind of guy, gave the two men gold in exchange for the chance to wear this unique suit that would be the best in the land. There was actually nothing real about this fabric, and the con artists were simply pretending to sew the suit. The "tailors" had the emperor try it on, and this was the moment when everyone saw the emperor had no clothes. Afraid of being thought of as ignorant, however, they all complimented the emperor and told him how wonderful he looked. Only an innocent child was honest and came forward. There wasn't one adult who was brave enough to say the truth for fear of what others would think.

This endearing tale epitomizes what I have seen happen in education throughout the years. It could be a teaching philosophy, a program, or a method; it really doesn't matter. If it is praised or promoted by an elite institution or backed by the gurus who know how to market their products well, everyone jumps on the bandwagon and is afraid to say the truth: "It doesn't work."

The thinking goes something like this – If X University says "This is the best," it must be. Then all the prestigious school districts want their teachers following this philosophy because it must be "the best." Of course, training is ongoing, follow-up is necessary, there are always books and materials that must be bought and updated regularly in order to be successful, and did I mention that there are certain assessment kits that should also go along with the program, and so on and so on. You get the idea.

And guess what happens? Who do you think does well and who struggles? The same children who were doing well continue to do well, and the children who were underperforming continue in the same vein. But the most stunning revelation is the reaction of the administrators who were expecting this to be the answer. They rationalize and make excuses: it must be the teachers' implementation; they didn't have enough training; the book choices are not matched correctly to the students; and the assessments are not driving instruction. I have heard them all. And everyone is afraid to say these words, "It doesn't work."

We try to fit a square peg into a round hole. We can try, and try again, but unless we are honest and brave, this malpractice will continue. We are a society believing in name-brand products and designer labels. There are programs and teaching frameworks that work, yet the decision makers will look down their noses at them because they are too basic and simple in theory. They are sold on prestige, and the beat goes on. Einstein said it best, "Few people are capable of expressing with equanimity opinions which differ from the prejudices of their social environment. Most people are incapable of forming such opinions."

Unfortunately, even when district administrators, building leaders, and teachers show courage and elect to try to change the status quo, implementing such change can often be frustrated by unforeseen setbacks.

LEADERSHIP: HOW ONE PERSON CAN MAKE OR BREAK A READING PROGRAM

When I was working as a Regional Reading Coach for a federally-funded grant, one of the districts I was assigned to was targeted due to low performance. This district had a transient population, many English Language Learners (ELL) (now known as English As A New Language), and many students receiving free or reduced lunch. With all the challenges, including poverty, the biggest hurdle, believe it or not, was the turnover in administration.

By the time the grant funds became available and we entered the district to begin our mission, the administrators who had sought out and applied for the grant were no longer there. Moreover, the new administration had hired an English Language Arts Coordinator who was schooled in whole language and leveled literacy, the antithesis of the grant's purpose. The grant was charged with bringing scientifically-based reading instruction into the early grades, K-3, to ensure that the children would receive best practices and become proficient readers by the end of third grade. The district, when applying for the grant, had agreed to abandon its existing reading program in favor of a program strong in phonological awareness and phonics, which was supported by the research. Either the district had not adequately explained to the new ELA Coordinator the implications of the grant before she accepted the position, or she did not fully appreciate the strict requirements imposed by the grant. She and I had many philosophical differences, but I assumed that over time she would become enlightened and see how science had paved the way for change. This did not happen.

My struggles with the ELA Coordinator continued, and she made it very difficult for me to do my job. The money she received from the grant for materials and professional development consistent with the grant's research and goals was spent instead on books and speakers promoting her views. She insisted upon dictating and controlling my schedule and access to the teachers and children, and she would conveniently forget to look at my requests for opportunities to model lessons in classrooms. At every turn in this district, I was faced with another barrier. I realized quickly that teachers have very little power, even if, as in this district, they want to utilize programs and methods that are instructionally sound. Some of the teachers loved the new information and wanted to implement the strategies, but they feared retaliation if they did not align themselves with the ELA Coordinator's views and teaching style. Teachers would see me in the lunchroom and express their frustration, but they felt they were caught in the middle of the Reading Wars.

I remember one attempt I made to have the ELA Coordinator hear a renowned speaker discuss the benefits of learning how to read words through a phonics-based approach. I invited her to attend the program with me in the hope that the message might be better received from an acclaimed expert in the field. She and I sat through the presentation, and I was thinking, "This is fabulous! I can't wait to hear what she says when it is over!" Well, what people believe is based on their perception. The two of us sat through the whole presentation, and she came away with an entirely different view of what was said. She heard only the parts that fit into her belief system and her take-away message was exactly what she wanted to hear. She was unchanged and even smug, as if her beliefs had been reinforced having attended the presentation. At that point, I knew that I had to "go through the back door" and reach the teachers differently.

My experience in that district taught me that attempting to make systemic change in a school, where educators are entrenched in their ways, can be challenging and, in some ways, unrealistic. The State Education Department tried to remind the district of its obligations under the agreement, yet the grant money was not taken away, and the district continued to implement practices that were not in the children's best interest. While some teachers recognized the value of evidence-based instruction and tried to utilize the strategies we provided, many of the teachers were only too happy to continue doing what they were doing. It was much easier. Whistle-blowers were ostracized and made to feel like they had done something wrong, even if it benefitted the children.

When we cannot speak up, and we have to follow a leader for fear of getting poor reviews or losing our jobs, the status quo continues. It is unfair to judge an initiative based on results that do not account for the commitment level of school leaders and district administrators. When we look at failing schools and low-performing districts, leadership is actually the most important ingredient and should never be overlooked. Democratic values are not always protected behind the school walls.

RESISTANT TEACHERS

"You must be the change you wish to see in the world." – *Mahatma Gandhi*

"Education is the most powerful weapon which you can use to change the world." – *Nelson Mandela*

Teachers expect children to grow, learn, and ultimately develop into flexible, thoughtful thinkers, ready to deal with adversity and be open to the possibility of change. Interestingly enough, many teachers are fearful of change and will go to extremes to protect their turf.

A stunning example of such resistance occurred with a seasoned teacher who had been teaching exactly the same lessons in the same grade for years. This particular teacher did not want a coach entering her classroom because she would then be expected to do something different, something she was not ready to do. I understood her fear and began working with other teachers who were more open to new strategies and ideas. I invited this teacher to join me in someone else's classroom to see how embedded coaching begins with the coach modeling lessons and the teacher observing. There should always be such collaboration between a coach and teacher before the teacher is expected to try anything new. It appeared that after seeing how I worked with her co-worker, the teacher was more willing to work with me; she had observed small, manageable changes, a little at a time.

I thought we had a breakthrough moment when we actually set a day and time for me to enter her classroom to begin working with her. I had prepared a lesson and brought my materials to her room at the scheduled time. To my surprise, I was not able to enter. She had hung a pocket chart over the window in the door to block any outside view and had all of her students sitting on the floor right in front of the door as she conducted a lesson. Looking through a small space in the window between the chart and the door frame, I waved to her to let her know I was outside. She shooed me away and pointed to her children as if to say it was not a good time. I knew this was a hopeless situation. This teacher had literally barricaded the door with human shields to protect herself. Change was not going to happen in that classroom.

Other less obvious signs of resistance occurred in every school, mainly with teachers who had been teaching for years. Such teachers would rather blame the children for their lackluster results than be reflective about their own practices. These are the teachers who, midway through a school year, still have books and materials sitting in their rooms sealed in shrink wrap, never opened. In one school, hands-on letter tiles, purchased and provided to the district through the grant, could not be located right before a workshop on how to use a particular program effectively. Nobody seemed to know what happened to the delivery. In a different building, the teacher created "a better way" to use the program that fit in with her standard lesson. She did not seem to care or want to understand that the program's effectiveness would be diminished if she did not use the program with fidelity.

One thing I learned visiting classrooms and working with teachers in many schools and districts is that teachers in isolation have no idea what their colleagues are doing behind closed doors. The instinct of teachers to believe that all teachers are working as hard as they are, or performing their duties adequately, is often fueled by solidarity. I think Gandhi would be disappointed if he expected all teachers to be the change they want to see in children. If education is our most powerful weapon, as Mandela so eloquently stated, how is it possible that so many educators would rather ignore reading research and instead place all the blame for the literacy crisis in this country on society, parents, and children?

ARE INDEPENDENT EXPERTS REALLY INDEPENDENT?

I was struck by an article I recently read about a popular breakfast cereal company's distinguished "Breakfast Council," a supposedly independent group of experts that helps the company with nutritional guidance. According to the article, the "independent" experts are paid by the company and given actual talking points such as, "I'm still feeling great from my bowl of cereal & milk this morning! [X Cereal is] my fave," as found on a Twitter chat. Another "expert" responded, without identifying herself, that she also loved [X Cereal] and posted a photo with her tweet. The article exposed that the company prohibited the experts from saying anything negative about the brand in exchange for payment of $13,000. Does this look like the behavior of an impartial group of experts giving you nutritional information? This council was used to teach continuing education classes to dieticians, publish academic papers, and influence the government's dietary guidelines. Is this information clearly explained to the public, the people who trust that an objective, qualified council is assessing the company's products honestly and fairly? I am bringing this to your attention because this "research" happens in all fields, especially in education.

I witnessed this firsthand when I was involved in the federally-funded literacy initiative. The grant money awarded to the local education agency was earmarked for many expenses: salaries, books and supplies, and, believe it or not, "research" on the work we were doing. The initiative was, in essence, paying an outside agency to write a report about the findings of our work. The initiative hired the researchers; the initiative conferenced with them; the initiative set up times for them to observe; and the initiative had the last say on what appeared in the report and how it should appear. As you can imagine, this did not make any sense to me. If we paid our own auditors and dictated the results, how could the report be unbiased? Well, it wasn't. Everyone involved in the grant answered survey questions that were kept anonymous, and somehow, the report did not reflect any of our input. The researchers conveniently ignored the negative and, instead, highlighted only what was authorized by the grant's director.

Numbers do not lie – people do. I believe in research, scientifically-based research, peer-reviewed, impartial, and replicable. But that is not necessarily what is valued or considered by our government or educators who want to use data to support an agenda. When I hear numbers thrown around at education conferences, I cannot help but think about how information and statistics can be skewed, and how publishing companies use this information to entice school districts to purchase products that are not aligned with what we know really works. There are all types of studies, and one needs to consider the independence, or lack thereof, of the panel of experts opining on the subject before deciding a program or product's worth.

The government, special interest groups, and our education system have let many children down by promoting and sustaining ineffective programs. It is easy to use a lack of money as an excuse for unsuccessful results. Unfortunately, if it were only a matter of money, that would be an easier fix than the problems that are so prevalent in our schools. Think of all the money wasted already.

THE "BEST" DISTRICTS, THE MOST TUTORS

L ong Island is one of the most segregated places to live and send children to school. According to recent surveys, Long Island has some of the best high schools in the country along with the highest per pupil spending. But we also have some of the lowest performing schools in New York State, and it is clearly delineated by the boundaries of poverty. There are some school districts that have repeatedly appeared on lists of failing schools, and the State continues to pour money into helping these districts succeed with very little recognizable improvements. It would appear that the school districts with the best reputations would have the best interventions and support services, and the low-performing school districts would have the least effective. Surprisingly, there is not much difference from one district to the other in terms of programs chosen and how they are being delivered.

Wealthier districts will be able to hire more specialists and keep groups smaller, an advantage that clearly helps struggling students. But there are excellent teachers in poverty-stricken areas and inferior teachers in wealthy districts, and many of the teachers across all districts have had the same training, professional development, programs, and materials. Why do some districts perform better than others?

Wealthier families will not sit back and wait for children to fail. They hire private tutors for everything. Reading, writing, math, honors courses, advanced placement courses, college entrance tests and essays, you name it, and they will have it for their children. Look at an upper middle-class or wealthy neighborhood and there are tutoring franchises on every block. In addition, there are independent tutors all over social media marketing their services. A poor community will not have private tutoring centers or independent tutors advertising. When the newspapers report the great scores on the ELA, Math, and high school exams, it does not factor in the extra hours of help, along with the expertise that some tutors bring to their subject matter. The high achieving districts get the credit for exemplary teaching, but this is not always the case. There are many low-performing districts that copy well-regarded districts and apply the same philosophy wondering why it worked elsewhere but not in their own district. They will blame teachers for poor implementation, and in some cases that is true. And, no doubt, children of educated parents living in affluent communities will have a head start in terms of vocabulary, experiences, and exposure to literature. But the elephant in the room is what money can buy, and it happens outside the walls of a school building.

PART II

QUEER LANGUAGE TO CLEAR LANGUAGE

<u>Our Queer Language</u>

When the English tongue we speak,
Why is 'break' not rhymed with 'freak'?
Will you tell me why it's true?
We say 'sew' but likewise 'few'?
And the maker of a verse,
Cannot cap his 'horse' with 'worse'?
'Beard' sounds not the same as 'heard',
'Cord' is different from 'word';
C-o-w is 'cow' but l-o-w is 'low';
'Shoe' is never rhymed with 'foe'.
Think of 'hose' and 'whose' and 'lose',
And think of 'goose' and yet of 'loose',
Think of 'comb' and 'tomb' and 'bomb';
'Doll' and 'roll' and 'home' and 'some';
And since 'pay' is rhymed with 'say',
Why not 'paid' with 'said', I pray?
We have 'blood' and 'food' and 'good',
Wherefore 'done' and 'gone' and 'lone'?
Is there any reason known?
And, in short, it seems to me,
Sounds and letters disagree.

This anonymous poem demonstrates the struggles of learning the English language. Although at least 85% of English words are decodable using phonics, the alphabetic code itself is complex. Other languages are

19

much easier to decipher because there is a one-to-one correspondence between letters and sounds. Many children do not just pick up learning how to read English; they need to be taught with a systematic, explicit, structured approach. While people say English is a "crazy language," with lots of exceptions to the rules, it is actually quite logical once the rules are made apparent.

ENGLISH AS A FOREIGN LANGUAGE

Did you ever try reading an article or book in a foreign language? I found myself in a library in Quebec, Canada's largest French speaking province, trying to kill an hour before a dinner reservation in La Roche, a trendy neighborhood on the rise, reminiscent of Williamsburg, Brooklyn or Astoria, Queens. I casually walked over to the magazine section, trying to read short, manageable articles in French. After all, French is one of the Romance languages, and I did take Spanish in school. How hard could it be? Well, I felt like a struggling reader – getting the gist through pictures, figuring out words in French through cognates (words in different languages that share a similar meaning, pronunciation, and spelling pattern), and piecing words together to "make meaning." The article, "Le Vin Est Bon Pour Vous," had a picture of a wine bottle on it and listed wine's many benefits. Somehow, I was able to understand that wine is good for you. I would not call what I did "deep reading," and I am sure I missed important information because I did not read many of the words accurately.

So this is what it is like to be functionally illiterate? I was painfully aware of my lack of literacy skills. It was certainly frustrating and could have been embarrassing if anyone asked me a question about the article. (Imagine how a child with reading difficulties feels when called upon in class.) I can only imagine how extremely difficult it would be to manage everyday life not fully comprehending the world, missing detailed information, and not being able to make independent decisions.

Thirty-two million people in this country are functionally illiterate, reading below a fifth grade level and not able to read well enough to apply for a job. It is unacceptable how many people go through school but cannot read beyond a basic level of literacy. There is no good reason why anyone, particularly your child, should feel like he or she is reading a foreign language and surrounded by words that have no meaning.

As you read on, you will discover how the current literacy practices in our schools are failing many children; yet, with the right instruction, English is not so mysterious after all.

THE FINNISH MYTH

Finland is universally ranked as having the top educational system in the world. Before Finnish children enter school, many attend a daycare program that builds skills they will need before formal schooling. Through teacher-directed play and free play, children learn how to problem-solve and think creatively. They are not bombarded with hours of homework and are not taught to read until age seven; in Finland, they know that the joy of learning is the most important prerequisite for later success.

Once Finnish children do begin learning how to read, however, it is much easier to teach them since there is a completely transparent alphabet code. This means that every word sounds exactly as it is written. When children learn the Finnish alphabet, they usually learn how to read quickly. Each letter has one sound, and only one sound. In English, this is not the case. We do not have a one-to-one correspondence between letters and sounds. The /s/ sound can be a letter S like in the word "snake" or the letter C like in the word "city." The /z/ sound can be the letter Z like in the word "zoo" or the letter S like in the word "nose." Also, two, three, and even four letters can represent one sound. The long /ō/ sound can be just an "o" as in no, or it can be /ō/ like in boat, row, toe, bone, and though. This can be so confusing when learning how to read English. Then, there can be the same letter team used for different sounds. For instance, look at the words, eat, bread, and steak. The "ea" vowel team has a different sound in each word.

We can all agree children need developmentally appropriate skills: active, hands-on learning, social-emotional development, self-regulation, and most importantly, time to play and explore. The United States should look to

Finland as an early childhood education model, particularly, the value and importance the Finnish people place on the crucial first six years of a child's life and the thought, attention, and funding they give to their daycare and primary school systems. However, it is unreasonable to compare American literacy rates with literacy rates in a country such as Finland. Because of the complexity of the English language, American children need much more time and practice to master the basics of learning how to read and write. Rather than overwhelm young children with content that is developmentally inappropriate, we need to slow down, teach thoroughly, build a strong foundation, let children master the alphabetic code, expand their vocabularies, and model spoken and written language. Only then can we expect American students to move through the public school system and become college and career ready.

STEP BY STEP

A trip to the Corning Museum in Corning, N.Y. provided me with more than just an appreciation of the art of glassmaking; it demonstrated a powerful analogy for learning just about anything. While watching the glass blowing demonstration, I could not help but think how logical learning is when we use a well-structured step-by-step plan.

Experienced glass blowers, called gaffers, develop their art over years of practice. It actually takes five years to be called a beginner! In order to become fluent, gaffers learn by working closely with a mentor and performing the steps repeatedly until muscle memory takes over and the actions become fluent. Inexperienced gaffers are choppy, tend to repeat steps, and reheat parts longer than their more experienced counterparts. When one makes a glass sculpture or vase, the base always comes first. If the base has a bubble or is uneven, all other steps that follow will be off. Clearly, it is very important to get the base steady. Although glass can be elastic and flexible, stressing the glass by heating and cooling too quickly will cause thermal shock and breakage. Above all, patience is necessary. In order to strengthen the glass, you need to go over it again and again.

As creative as it is, glassblowing is not only an art, it is a science, and it is a skill learned in a systematic, structured way. It is taught through mentorship, not haphazardly. If this all seems like common sense, then why is it that we expect something very different from children learning to read? Emergent readers are fragile readers; like young gaffers, we cannot rush them through the process of developing their skills without first ensuring their proficiency in the basics. Otherwise, "bubbles" will develop in the foundation, putting children on shaky ground.

WHERE TO BEGIN? TEACHING LETTER NAMES OR SOUNDS?

Across the country, children are taught the ABC song at a very young age. Research confirms that knowing the letter names is a strong predictor for learning to read. But do we really need to know the names of letters when we read or do we need to know their sounds? We certainly need to recognize the letters when we see them, but identifying each by name is not necessary when we learn to read; the sounds, however, are critical, and many educators, especially in the United Kingdom, which is also attempting to raise literacy levels after years of failed policies, believe that teaching letter names should come only after a firm foundation in understanding the sounds that correspond to the letters is established. In the USA, letter names are definitely taught by most parents and teachers first, yet, when we stop and think about it, we blend sounds, not letter names, to make words.

The first time I read about this approach was in the Diane McGuinness book I mentioned in an earlier chapter, Why Our Children Can't Read and What We Can Do About It. The McGuinness method, Linguistic Phonics, is an approach to reading and spelling that builds on speech. Children begin by listening to familiar words and learning to identify individual sounds in the words. These individual sounds (known as phonemes) have corresponding "sound pictures" or letters (called graphemes) that correspond to the sounds in language. For example, the word "boat" has three individual sounds represented by the letters B-OA-T. McGuinness believes that since our written language was developed as a way to code oral language, children should be taught in the same direction - from speech to print. She argues that teaching letter names is confusing to children and should be avoided. She also does not believe in teaching the rules of spelling and syllabication, the division of words into syllables, either in speech or in writing. McGuinness feels the linguistic phonics approach will prevent bad habits from developing and break the habits of guessing and whole word memorization.

A sound to print phonics program that utilizes this approach is Phono-Graphix. I became a Phono-Graphix Reading Therapist before becoming a certified Wilson Dyslexia Practitioner and had great success with this method. Through the years, I have explored, trained, and utilized other methods as well. Although I have discovered that not all phonics programs are created equal, all strong phonics programs do have one common feature – they explicitly teach the alphabetic code from the bottom up. Whether or not a program uses spelling or syllabication rules is not the main issue; rather, it is the teaching of reading in a structured, organized way that is sensible for the student that makes the difference.

Knowing the names of the letters may be a strong predictor of early reading success, but it could also mean that alphabet name recognition simply correlates with, rather than causes, early reading success. Children can be successful learning to read with or without beginning with letter names, but they absolutely need an understanding of sound and letter correspondences.

A "SOUND" FOUNDATION

Many of you know the meaning of phonics (the relationship between letters and sounds) believing it is the first step in learning how to read. Although it is one of the building blocks for reading, there is something that is even more fundamental; it is called phonemic awareness, the ability to hear, identify, and manipulate individual sounds in words. When children learning to read possess phonemic awareness, they will be able to connect letters to sounds. Without phonemic awareness, phonics instruction will not be effective. For example, if I wanted to teach a child how to spell the word "clock," he first needs to **hear** the individual sounds (phonemes) AND THEN apply letter-sound correspondence. There are four individual sounds in the word clock - /k/ /l/ /ŏ/ /k/, and then the corresponding letters are matched — c-l-o-ck. Without first being able to hear and identify individual sounds, phonics, which is the coding of letters to those sounds, would not make sense. It is not possible to match letters to sounds that are not heard. Some educators believe that phonemic awareness needs to be taught separately from phonics, while others believe that it is best to teach it at the same time. Which way is correct?

Having worked with many children with learning challenges, phonemic awareness can be extremely difficult, particularly for those children with language-based disabilities such as auditory processing disorder and dyslexia.

Instruction in phonemic awareness begins with teaching children to hear bigger units of oral language. For example, recognizing the separation of words in sentences and syllables in words, or listening for the rhyme in pairs of words while also recognizing which words do not sound alike are all listening skills that fall under the umbrella term, phonological awareness. Preschool educators work with children to develop an "ear" for hearing words and syllables using nursery rhymes, clapping out words, and facilitating listening activities. Parents can help their children become aware of sounds and recognize similar and different sounds by engaging in rhyming games and songs. Children's television always offers rhymes and songs that include the manipulation of sounds through simplistic, catchy tunes that develop this important foundational skill for reading.

Many listening programs and apps for the computer have been created and marketed for the sole purpose of helping children develop an "ear" for sound; however, results have been mixed and many schools that have piloted these computer-based programs soon realize they wasted time and money. In Gainsville, Florida, the Gainsville Sun newspaper article dated November 6, 2016, "1.2 Million Dollar Reading Program Produces Weak Results," illustrates how Alachua Public Schools and other districts will not continue to fund these costly programs.

When it comes time to begin to teach a child to read, the most effective way to show that letters are a written code for sounds is to teach phonemic awareness at the same time as letter recognition. Children do not always make the connection between sounds and letters if phonemic awareness and phonics are taught separately. It would be like teaching the steps to driving a car without the car; it might help to know what to do, but there is nothing like actually doing it. Once children can hear the individual sounds in words, explicitly teaching sound and letter correspondence should begin immediately.

There will be times when children will need more instruction in hearing the sounds in our language. The more sounds and syllables that are blended together in long words, the harder they are to detect separately. This skill not only affects reading, it affects spelling and writing as well. Try to imagine spelling a word that is either difficult for you or not used very often in your writing. You will first try to "see" the word in your mind's eye. Next, you will start to say the word in chunks (syllables), and finally, you will write letters that you think correspond to each sound within each chunk. This is much more difficult than reading because the letters are not in front of you. Without internalizing the sounds that make up a word, every word that you spell would rely completely on visual memory. Some children can intuitively pick up the connection between sounds and letters, while others need a direct approach. If phonics is taught without explicitly developing an awareness of sounds, it might not be effective.

DYSLEXIA OR DYS"TEACH"IA

According to the International Dyslexia Association (IDA), dyslexia is defined as "a specific learning disability that is neurobiological in origin. It is characterized by difficulties with accurate and/or fluent word recognition and by poor spelling and decoding abilities." The key word is "neurobiological," an illness of the nervous system caused by genetic or biological factors.

In a classroom, teachers might witness the following: children with average to above average intelligence struggling to read, write, and spell, frustrated by schoolwork, and choosing not to read independently, all of which inhibit vocabulary growth and overall reading comprehension. But is every child struggling to read, write, and spell dyslexic? Can we honestly say that so many children have learning disabilities? Isn't it possible that children are just not being taught with a system that allows for smooth learning of the alphabetic principle? Could it be that the balanced literacy programs used in schools are not as balanced as we would hope? Could it actually be what many of us refer to as "dysteachia," poor or inadequate teaching which results in poor reading, writing, and spelling that can look like a learning disability?

If we look at how reading is taught in kindergarten and first grade, it can look very different across the country. Many children are taught with what is commonly called a Balanced Literacy approach. This "balance" supposedly includes phonemic awareness, phonics, fluency, vocabulary, and comprehension, the components of literacy. Within this framework, children are matched to leveled books that range in difficulty, and children are guided in small groups to use "word-solving" strategies. Phonics can either be taught implicitly through the text or through a separate phonics program used in addition to the leveled readers. Other schools may use a basal reader with sequential lessons that build cumulatively to address all five components: phonemic awareness, phonics, fluency, vocabulary, and comprehension.

So, what can go wrong? In the first instance, the "word-solving" strategies are based on a "cueing system." Instead of reading words, children are encouraged to use cues in the context to figure them out. This method actually encourages children to jump around the page to figure out how to read words, which frequently results in guessing. If anyone has seen the beginner books in a leveled literacy approach, one will see that the pictures and repetitive use of "sight" words or memorized words will basically give the story away. There really is very little need for phonics to be used. So even if phonics is being taught, and I say that loosely since there are many ways to teach phonics, children will not be using this skill to read and will not get practice in understanding the sound-symbol connection. The phonics program of choice becomes an isolated exercise when combined with guided reading and the strategies that are espoused in a leveled literacy approach. In essence, the children are not so much "reading" as guessing with a little help from cues.

The creators of such phonics programs will say that their programs can be used with any reading program because they want to sell them, and they know that schools are not going to discard their existing programs. Tons of money has been spent on supplemental phonics programs, only to see them relegated to a secondary role as part of a balanced approach. I have been in many classrooms as a regional literacy coach, working with teachers, building literacy coaches, and administrators, and there is a misunderstanding that permeates schools. Most educators are professional, well-meaning, and dedicated; however, there is a hodge-podge of contradictions in an effort to be balanced.

Unfortunately, the training that children receive at the beginning of their schooling is how their brains will learn to read. Since reading is not natural like learning to talk, children who do not pick up how to read when exposed to print will struggle. These are the children who do not intuitively understand the rules of spelling; they continue to use inventive spelling beyond first grade and cannot even correct themselves because they do not know how to judge what looks right. Without handwriting instruction, these are the children who figure out what letters "kinda" look like, and draw the letters from the bottom up, or worse, have different starting points until it looks correct. These are the children who write poorly and only use simplistic words that are in their sight vocabulary.

Are all these children dyslexic? If children are not being taught properly, they can appear dyslexic. Is dyslexia real? Of course it is! But many children fall through the cracks that would otherwise not have these difficulties if they were taught with a complete phonetic system and learned reading, spelling, and writing with direct, explicit instruction.

What does "explicit" instruction look like? It is not ambiguous; children are given a direct model of instruction and clearly know each step. They are engaged and active learners. They are not left to guess what they should do. The teacher monitors progress and makes adjustments as needed. The teacher does not assume children are picking up skills without seeing evidence of learning through interaction. Robert was a casualty of indirect, whole language teaching philosophy. He never just "picked up" how to read.

BUILDING THE FOUNDATION

My husband and I have been taking ballroom dance lessons for quite some time. We began with a set of introductory lessons through a very popular franchised studio. New students usually are given the newest instructors, and we were no different. Our first instructor was actually an advanced student at the school who decided to give lessons to beginners. This particular school is noted for adhering to a strict syllabus, yet this new instructor chose to depart from the structured method. I will never forget our first salsa lesson; he began teaching us "Cuban Motion," proper hip movement caused by bending and straightening the knees. This difficult hip action usually is taught after basic steps have been mastered. This "teacher" happened to have been an excellent dancer, but clearly he was not ready to give lessons. He told us that we would just be able to pick up the steps easily. Yeah, right.

Shortly after a few lessons, he left and we had a series of teachers who ranged in skill level and experience. One teacher was quite good, but she was auditioning for acting and dancing roles in NYC and canceled on us quite a bit. Another instructor had an excellent background, was a dance major in college and classically trained in ballet. She was a wonderful person and teacher; however, she was relatively new to ballroom dance and relied on the syllabus and teaching videos to stay ten steps ahead of us. She feared deviating from the curriculum and checked off each step as taught. We were learning a lot of steps, but those steps did not help us feel confident and natural when dancing outside the studio or with the school's more advanced students. We ended up taking a break from dancing and never returned to this school.

After a while, one of our friends recommended our present instructor,

Lisa Sparkles in Syosset, NY. Lisa, a former professional dancer, worked for various schools and learned from excellent teachers in the dance community. She also invested in her own professional development and was able to gather the best teaching strategies to use with her students. Lisa intuitively understands strong teaching methods: repetition with cyclical review, positive feedback, error correction, and pushing us just beyond our comfort level without reaching frustration (although my husband might disagree with the last point).

Good teaching is good teaching. Whether one is learning a sport, playing an instrument, or learning how to read, students learn best from someone who is experienced, knowledgeable, enthusiastic, and understands how to individualize instruction. As an educator, I appreciate those qualities, even more so now being an adult learner in a new situation. Learning to dance has been fun but humbling, and it has made me a better teacher. My husband, a natural athlete who easily picks up sports, but sometimes struggles at dance, also seemed to recognize the connection, once saying, "Every parent, teacher, and coach should try to learn something new like this and see what it's like to walk in the shoes of a struggling student." I couldn't agree more.

CAN SCIENTIFICALLY RESEARCH-BASED READING PROGRAMS GUARANTEE SUCCESS?

While posting on social media, a member of a particular group responded with this comment:

"I am asking the question I ask of all trained/certified instructors of reading approaches such as OG, Barton and Wilson, so please don't be offended. Can you please share with us what independently conducted research--not post hoc or surveys, or studies-- but matched subject samples by demographics of test subjects and control subjects that shows the program's efficacy in short and long term gains and in what areas those were observed and if whether the research was conducted in school settings or a controlled setting. I know I am asking a lot, but this kind of research is essential in selecting an appropriate intervention and knowing that it can be replicated in a school setting or if progress can only be accomplished in a specialized environment. Thank you for your time and reply."

I am sharing this with you because I feel these are valid questions that many others might be asking. Are scientifically research-based reading programs able to guarantee success for all? Absolutely not! But it is crucial to use evidence-based teaching strategies and practices if we are going to help children with language-based learning difficulties succeed. Below are other factors which must be considered:

• Expertise of the Teacher – Is the teacher properly trained to execute the program? Does the teacher "buy-in" to the program or is the program being forced on the teacher? Does the teacher have enough knowledge about how to gauge progress and understand how to individualize without destroying the program's effectiveness? Does the program require training and certification to be able to use it effectively or can anyone pick up a manual and begin teaching?

• Setting – Is the program's research conducted in a classroom environment or is it controlled? Is the research showing success for small group or one-on-one instruction? Can it be used with the same effectiveness in any setting?

• Demographics – Is there a cross section of children in the research study? Are children from the inner-city, suburbs, or rural parts of the country? Is English their first language? Do they receive free lunch? Are they mostly Caucasians or African Americans? Did their parents complete high school or are they highly educated?

• Time – How often will the child receive services? How long will the sessions be? Is the intervention given enough time during the week to see the expected progress? Is the program being watered down so that there is a "balance" in a school's balanced literacy curriculum?

Vendors will claim that their programs work and will present data supporting these claims; however, all factors need to be taken into consideration. Rarely do administrators take the time to visit schools with the same demographics to see if the program they are considering is working. Rarely do schools pilot a program before adopting it for the whole school. Usually, a consultant for the program is hired to help with the implementation, and the most important factor, the teacher, is overlooked. Even if a school district does its own research to explore the evidence-based program, and even if the program has, in fact, been peer reviewed and demonstrates gains, it does not always account for how the program will be implemented and by whom. Demographics and group size are not always clearly stated.

Parents can fight for "systematic, structured, sequential, repetitive, phonologically-based" programs and sadly not see the results that they had hoped for. Programs do not teach children, teachers do.

HISTORY REPEATS ITSELF

I remember learning to read with the look-say method books, Fun with Dick and Jane. "Run, Spot, run! Run, run, run!" It was 1971 in New York City, and I was in first grade. This reading program was extremely popular during that time, and I remember my first grade teacher, Mrs. Reiner, drawing word family houses on the chalkboard to show us how the –un family had the following words living in their house – run, fun, sun, and gun. Somehow, I learned that ton, won, one, and done did not live in that house, even though it was not explained to me. I was fortunate to be able to pick up reading through seeing words and making associations. Not everyone is so lucky. In first grade, I did not realize that many of my classmates must have struggled with this approach.

Another popular reading teaching method utilized in the 70s was the use of a tachistoscope, a big metal projector, reminiscent of the old movie cameras. The tachistoscope was meant to increase fluency and reading comprehension. The device, used for the whole class, would reveal a window of words in phrases, building up to sentences, and increasing in speed to encourage us to read words grouped together rather than one word at a time. Looking back, it seems strange that this could be useful for a whole class. We all have different reading rates, so how could the machine account for these differences? I am sure there were children sitting in the class not getting a thing out of the words moving across the board. They probably were thankful the lights were closed so they could zone out for a while.

When I look back at my elementary reading instruction, it is easy to understand how some children advanced to honors English courses and did quite well, while others barely got through school. As I said, I was one of the fortunate ones, able to read, spell, and write easily, and I always landed in the "One" class. (Tracking was common in those days.) It really didn't matter what curriculum was used for children who could pick up the alphabetic code easily. But I know of many other children who went through school, always in the bottom tier classes and relegated to low level coursework. These children were doomed from the start. I see now, though, that it was all about how they were taught. If these children were given proper instruction, their lives could have been different.

Interestingly enough, we have not learned much over the years. We still expect children to learn through sight words, predictable text, and guided reading books. We encourage them to read "fluently" before they even know how to read accurately. Even though teachers today are more engaged during small group instruction, the children in the lower performing groups are still not getting their needs met and remain on a track that does not seem to take them where they need to go.

SIGHT WORDS CAN ACTUALLY BE DETRIMENTAL FOR BEGINNER READERS

Although English is a phonetic language, there is still a school of thought that wants children to memorize a certain number of words by the time they finish kindergarten. Some people would argue and say that it can't hurt, or it is part of a "Balanced Literacy" program. But I would say it is actually extremely damaging while children are learning sound and symbol correspondence.

Kindergarten students are expected to see that letters represent and map to the sounds in our language, and they will eventually learn that there is not always a transparent match. Sometimes there are multiple sounds for a combination of letters and other times there are multiple letter combinations used to represent one sound. For instance, the sound /oe/ like in the word "toe" can have a number of possible letter combinations for the sound. Boat, rope, no, row, and though use different letters corresponding to the same sound. Also, there could be more than one sound for a combination of letters. The "ow" in row, know, and window, can be how, now, brown, and cow, representing the /ou/ sound.

If reading is taught sequentially, cumulatively, and directly, most children will be reading by the end of first grade. However, if sight words are stressed in the early grades without the skill of "sounding out" a word being ingrained as the primary strategy for word reading, many students will begin to use whole word reading as the preferred strategy. Some educators support whole word reading on the grounds that some children are visual learners, and using sight words should be just another way to access print. Why then is sight word reading a problem?

One reason for not getting into the habit of memorizing words is it stifles children from reading many more words utilizing phonics. Once children understand the alphabetic principle, there will be unlimited words at their disposal. If they continue to think of reading as a memorization task, they will be limited by how many words are taught and remembered throughout the school year.

It is also confusing to learn phonics and sight words at the same time. Adults view this differently from young children. Adults believe that children will need sight words to help them become fluent readers. This is not the case as the content becomes more complicated and the words are not in their sight vocabulary. Many children start believing that all words can be memorized and stop trying to sound out. Struggling readers might be successful with this technique in the early grades because the text structure is simple and the words are relatively easy to figure out based on the pictures and context. If they continue to think that this will serve them well in the upper grades, they begin to see quickly that this is a flawed strategy. This is when the guessing habits start, "comprehension" issues arise, and they choose not to read for pleasure.

Many educators will stress the importance of both types of learning, phonics and sight word reading. This is usually a diplomatic way to satisfy everyone; give a healthy balance of a few different strategies. I don't believe this is the answer. The message to young children should be that some words have something a little different that we need to look at carefully. The Wilson Reading System, a well-known intervention program, calls sight words, "trick" words. There are actually very few words that are not decodable (able to be sounded out using phonics). Usually, parts of a word can be phonetically figured out and only a small part of the word is truly tricky. Giving children instruction that sends the message to read "all through the word from left to right" rather than memorizing the words should be the default strategy for children.

For many children, the different strategies will not matter and they will learn to read without a problem. But for 20% of new readers, the way reading is taught makes a world of difference. Instead of this so-called "balanced literacy" approach which leaves so many children behind and in need of intervention to catch up, perhaps a more structured, explicit approach for everyone would level the playing field from the start, providing all children with a solid foundation. The children who can learn to read with any method still benefit from understanding how words work, as evidenced by better spelling and writing skills.

JULIE

Julie was new to the district when she started 5th grade. She was assigned to an AIS group based on her dismal assessment scores and teacher recommendation. Her 4th grade end-of-year report card from her old school did not reflect her classroom performance or reading ability, which is quite typical when working with transient students. It seems as though there is never a paper trail to document interventions and progress when children have not stayed in a school very long. I think the hope is that someone else will notice a problem and deal with it. Julie was clearly a victim of that mindset. There is absolutely no way her learning issues could have gone unnoticed.

Julie came to my class right after lunch every other day for reading help. Rubbing her eyes and squinting, she was supposed to wear glasses for reading but never had them with her. Each day, I would ask her about the glasses, and I would hear that her mother was going to take her to the optician to get a new pair. I wrote a letter to her mother but didn't receive a response. Then I tried calling home, and I still did not get an answer. Finally, Julie walked into the room wearing her glasses, with a big smile, and pointed to her face. I was very pleased to see that she came prepared to read; unfortunately, the glasses did not make a difference. With or without glasses, Julie had severe reading problems.

I knew this child needed more help than the others. I asked her if she would meet with me during her recess time for about twenty minutes every other day, and I would give up prep time to work with her one-on-one. With my principal's permission, I began teaching her basic phonics and used decodable readers to reinforce the alphabetic principle. Decodable readers are used to practice the phonics principles taught and are meant for

41

the sole purpose of learning the alphabetic code automatically. Decodable readers are the "training wheels" for gaining confidence as a reader. She would take home the book, practice, and return it to me at our next session. Julie started to make progress once she understood how to blend sounds together into words. Julie had no support at home and practiced on her own with my guidance. She had a strong desire to improve, and her positive attitude was a real asset.

Meanwhile, I was getting a lot of pressure from Julie's homeroom teacher to recommend testing for special education. I was convinced, however, that Julie did not have a learning problem since she learned quickly. She just needed the right intervention in a one-on-one setting to begin to close the gap. It is shocking to think that she was passed on through the grades for years without anyone trying to help her. She continued the following year in AIS, and she began passing her tests for the first time. There wasn't a time that I walked in the hall and didn't hear her scream, "Ms. Borkowsky!" Julie would always run over, give me a hug, and smile as if I were her best friend.

WHEN READING COMPREHENSION BEGINS

Try reading the passage below. Is it difficult for you to understand? Believe it or not, this is what it looks like when a child reads with 91% accuracy. That might seem high, but is it enough to comprehend?

When he saw Jan, dkfjkdjfk just keheddld and decided to leave the building. She has been dhfuvkehd and that was not all. She has also fjvmdkej the proposal and told Jan to dkcidllddl. What a shock! It was time to do something about that. He felt cmbcdit and rjtuhrap. Who could blame him? He called his friend, Joe, and the two of them went to djcdjiek for a drink. Later that night, his dhfidke asked him to have a much needed talk with her, and that was all he could take. Why did this have to be such a hard day?

When children do not read with 98% accuracy, it affects their comprehension. How can they understand fully what they are reading when words are either left out or misread? This might be misdiagnosed as a comprehension issue if the child is reading silently and answers questions incorrectly. As you can see, the core issue in this case is decoding. If the child cannot lift the words off the page, he or she will not derive meaning. Viewing this solely as a comprehension problem overlooks the root cause.

While the goal of reading instruction is always comprehension, systematic phonics instruction must occur in the primary grades and be taught thoroughly to form the foundation for comprehension. "There is no comprehension strategy powerful enough to compensate for the fact that you can't read the words," stated Dr. Anita Archer in her excellent book, *Explicit Instruction.* If there are gaps in children's understanding of the alphabetic principle, it will affect their performance in the upper grades. We can all agree that reading without meaning lacks purpose, and writing without coherent ideas is meaningless. Once foundational skills are mastered and stored in long term memory, the brain can be actively engaged to read for comprehension.

Children just learning to read are usually excited to get started. For many children, however, learning to read quickly becomes a struggle. Some of these children may just need more time to mature; others may not be able to hear the sounds in language. In either case, children may turn away from the learning process, frustrated as they see their classmates advancing, while they are not keeping up. It is the moment when children go from "unconscious incompetence," not being aware of learning deficiencies, to "conscious incompetence," being fully aware that they have fallen behind their peers.

Such children may begin to hide their learning issues in a number of ways. The class clown will bring negative attention upon himself to mask what he is feeling; after all, being a bad child is preferable to being seen as a stupid child. Some children try to disappear; they play with their pencils and look down, hoping the teacher won't see them. Still others will "pretend" read; those are the children who sound like readers but are merely filling in blanks based on their limited knowledge of a book and by using pictures and other cues to act like they know what is going on. These children are usually quite good at fooling others into thinking they are progressing.

Children do not like to be wrong and will do everything possible to hide their mistakes. It is not unusual for children to purposely write two different answers and have the teacher try to decipher which one was meant to be chosen. Instead of narrowing down choices and trying to make sense of what is being asked, they write in a manner that is not understandable and try to explain their choice after the correct answers are revealed. How can we help children break the habits of guessing, impulsivity, and indecisiveness?

If children are fortunate enough to receive the right intervention, they will begin to crack the alphabetic code and see how 44 sounds in the English language correspond to 26 letters and the combinations that represent them. This does not happen overnight. Learning and committing the alphabetic code to memory takes substantial guided practice and feedback to develop new pathways in the brain. Struggling readers receiving such assistance will reach the "conscious competence" stage, where they know what they should be doing, but it will not yet be natural for them. They can read accurately for the most part, but move slowly through text, self-correcting errors, and expending a lot of energy. You might notice your child yawning or looking exhausted while reading. Imagine trying to comprehend complex material when reading so cautiously.

Through practice and cyclical review, most children will begin to automatically know what to do and attain the next stage, "unconscious competence." Provided a child has a decent vocabulary and core knowledge about a topic, once an adequate fluency rate is achieved, the child will be able to read with ease, not think about every step in order to recognize words and phrases, and comprehend more of what is being read.

The problem lies in how the difficulty is remedied. Many schools will either not recognize the children who need help or will recognize the children but not offer the right services to match the need. One of the classic examples of good intentions gone wrong and how struggling students did not get services aligned with their needs was Reading Recovery (RR), a prevalent program that became popular in this country in the 1980s, and which many school districts saw as the answer for struggling first grade students. There were positive attributes to the Reading Recovery program: one-on-one instruction given to emergent readers, one half-hour session, four days a week for half the school year, and RR was supposed to be for the weakest students. However, in reality, very few students could be chosen for RR since it was designed to be one-on-one; it was extremely expensive to implement since it required a certified teacher and accommodated very few children; and the methods used were not phonics-based, systematic, explicit, and direct. Moreover, the lowest performing students were frequently not chosen because of poor behavior, inattention, or lack of family involvement.

In fact, the selection process under RR illustrates how data and its conclusions can be corrupted. After children were assessed using an Early Literacy Profile (ELP), the RR teacher would tally the results and "carefully" look at the lowest performers in all first grade classrooms. Then, the RR teacher would conference with each classroom teacher about possible candidates for the program. Since "Little Books" were to be sent home with the children in plastic baggies for practice and were required to be returned the next day, it was important that the "right" children were chosen. If a child was not "suitable" based on anticipated outcomes, the child would be bypassed in favor of a child who had a better chance at being successful. These variables were not included in the Reading Recovery data results, which were skewed in a positive direction. Also, "success" depended on parent participation to review the word-solving strategies and picture-driven cueing that were taught during the RR lesson. Based on this criteria, the chosen children appeared to do quite well because the easy, leveled books had pictures that basically gave away the story. As these same children got older, these ineffective strategies did not work when words became harder, the content more complex, and pictures were removed. Many of these "graduates" of RR would return to Academic Intervention Services and many became students I tutored privately when they got to second, third, or fourth grade

Some schools offer interventions that could work but do not effectively take children through the different stages until mastery is achieved. Children receiving remediation in school frequently do not get enough practice, error correction, and positive feedback to change the pathways in the brain to accommodate the new learning. Poor implementation of intervention programs is a common cause for continued failure in the upper grades.

There are many fine programs meant for struggling readers with language-based difficulties. The common characteristics of such programs are phonologically-based, sequential, structured, systematic, and repetitive instruction, with multiple practice opportunities to build new neural pathways in the brain. A child with or without an Individualized Education Program (IEP) will benefit from Wilson, Phono-Graphix, SRA, or any other program if, and only if, it is implemented with fidelity, taught by a trained professional, and monitored by someone who understands the needs of this type of learner. In the public school system, this is usually not the case.

A principal's main concern is, understandably, to have as many children serviced as possible. I have seen groups of eight to twelve students receiving "intensive" instruction. That size is way too large to meet the needs of students with difficulties. The schedule also might not allow for children to be seen every day, especially in districts with many low-performing students. Throw in the assembly performances, trips, fire drills, and other special days, such as "Movie Day" right before a holiday, and before you know it, the children have received very little worthwhile time on task.

Moreover, the reading teacher or special education teacher may or may not have had training in implementing the specialized program, or, even worse, may decide to pick and choose the parts that are easy to use and leave out the "multisensory" part. I remember meeting teachers who did not want to bother taking out the letter tiles to build words since, according to them, "it was a waste of time" and their students just "played" with the tiles. There are also teachers who do not enjoy using a program because they find it boring, even if it is beneficial for the student. It is much more fun to have a "literature circle" and read "real" books.

Meanwhile, parents are left to wonder why their child is not making progress. They assume, as do many administrators and teachers, the program is not working. Well, I ask you, do you think it is the program or the implementation of the program? This is not what intervention should look like. I can honestly say, having worked as a regional reading coach in districts across Long Island, and as a tutor for children from some of the highest performing ones, this scenario is all too common.

Parents need to be aware that no program or teacher can work magic. I tell all my clients that I am not a magician; we need to work together and there needs to be a commitment to practicing often. Any teacher or tutor who tells you otherwise is misguided. The key to success is through knowledge, and when parents know the process and how much work it takes, the chances of a successful outcome are far greater. This does not mean that children cannot succeed without an involved parent or caregiver; it just means that without adequate practice and home support, progress will be slower and children may stay in the "conscious competence" stage much longer before reaching unconscious competence. When parents carve out a portion of the day to practice the skills taught and reinforce the concepts, there is a better chance that their children will learn to effortlessly decode words and better understand what they are reading. And that is where true reading comprehension begins.

MORE QUEER LANGUAGE

It seems as though the English language delights as well as baffles us. Singular and plural nouns can be really challenging for someone learning the English language. Should I add an "s," "es," or change the form of the word? Sometimes, the word is just left alone, as in sheep, deer, moose, fish, and shrimp, all of which are both singular and plural. The poem below exemplifies this difficulty.

We'll begin with box, and the plural is boxes,
But the plural of ox is oxen, not "oxes"
Then one fowl is a goose not geese,
Yet the plural of moose would never be "meese,"

You may find a lone mouse or a whole lot of mice,
But the plural of house is houses, not "hice."
If the plural of man is always men,
Why shouldn't the plural of pan be "pen"?

Cow in the plural may be cows or kine.
But the plural of vow is vows not "vine."
I speak of a foot and you show me your feet.
I give you a boot; would you call a pair "beet"?
If the singular is tooth and the plural is teeth,
Why shouldn't the plural of booth be "beeth"?
If the singular is this, and the plural is these,
Should the plural of kiss rightly be "keese"?

Then, with ONE you use that and with THREE, those,
Yet the plural of hat is never called "hose."
We speak of a brother and also of brethren;
But though we say mother, we never say "methren."

The masculine pronouns are he, his, and him,
But imagine the feminine as she, "shis," and "shim."
So English, I think -- and you must agree --
Is a language as queer as any you'll see.

CAN YOUR CHILD REALLY READ?

How can you be sure if your child knows how to read? This is a question I am asked all the time. If you just hear your child read familiar books with predictable text, you might not be able to tell. Many young children memorize their favorite stories and "read" aloud to entertain their parents and family members. Pictures reinforce that they are reciting the story correctly. As they get older, their sight word recognition grows, and they are able to fool others into believing that they are reading, even themselves. But when you really pay attention, you notice that words are altered based on what the child thinks is the word, not what is actually on the page. Small, familiar words such as "in" and "on" are left out or confused, multi-syllable words such as "continent" and "content" are guessed at based on the beginning and ending syllables, and words that don't look anything alike are substituted for one another based on contextual cueing.

Here is a quick and easy way to see if you have cause for concern: Have your child read a list of words that are not common and see what happens. Try one syllable words first such as brute, strip, rude, hoe, foe, raw, haul, maul, and then multi-syllable words such as contrast, consonant, expansive, and inconsistently. Some children will have no problem reading isolated words, even ones that are not in their vocabularies yet. For others, it will reveal if they have problems with blending sounds, recognizing vowel teams, and breaking up long words. Strong readers will have the skill to chunk the words into decodable parts and figure them out. They will also be able to process words quickly. On the other hand, the less skilled reader will read slowly, not having an understanding of how to chunk the word or recognize the vowel sounds, and they might not even bother trying if the word is challenging.

Try to vary the structural elements of the smaller words; include words that have consonant blends (such as flap, prop, and mist) and vowel teams or diphthongs (such as pearl, fawn, coil, and gown). For older children, give them multisyllabic words with different prefixes and suffixes (joyous; joyously; joyfully; joyless), and see how they do. Don't be surprised if they actually can read these words better than some of the smaller words; sometimes, they will pay more attention to a longer word simply because it forces them to go slower through the word. If you have any doubt, your instincts are probably correct. In speaking with many parents throughout the years, they are usually the first ones to suspect reading difficulties.

Some words are frequently confused by even the strongest readers. For example, a word such as "thorough" will sometimes be read as "through," "though," or "thought." Even with contextual clues, the word "thorough" can be misread, although it is less likely to happen when the reader can self-correct based on the surrounding words or thoughts.

Try it now – "The police officers performed a **thorough** investigation at the crime scene." Even if the reader does not know the meaning of "thorough," the sentence carries a lot of meaning.

Strong readers can read isolated words by sounding out and recalling a familiar word. But what if you try this experiment and realize that while your child can read words individually, she cannot read the same words smoothly when placed in passages? What is that information telling you?

When your child has no apparent problems with decoding and can identify words in isolation, but cannot read those same words easily in a passage, it could be a visual tracking problem. What happens if an index card is placed under a line of text? Is your child able to read better? By blocking out other words on the page, is she more comfortable? Is it easier to read shorter lines of text than longer lines?

If a child has difficulty with visual tracking, you might notice reduced fluency when reading aloud. You might also notice your child skipping lines of text when her eyes sweep back to begin a new line. Does your child move her whole head instead of just the eyes moving from left to right? Do you see your child tilting her head to read in an awkward posture, almost as though she is napping while reading? Does your child point to each word? These are just some of the more noticeable signs of a visual tracking problem that could be holding your child back if phonics is not the root cause.

MAYBE IT IS A READING COMPREHENSION PROBLEM

Have you heard your child complain about reading, homework, and studying? "I don't understand this." "I can't remember what happened." "Why do I have to read this again and again?" "I hate this book." "This is so stupid." Then, have you met with your child's teacher and heard comments such as: "X doesn't pay attention to the details," "X tries very hard, but doesn't seem to understand the main idea," "X needs to work harder and apply himself," or the standard, "X is making progress; give it time"? In my thirty years as a teacher, reading specialist, tutor, and literacy coach to other teachers, I have heard them all. The list goes on and on, and yet I constantly hear parents say they still don't understand why their child struggles.

As mentioned above, strong readers are able to read isolated words while struggling readers might guess or confuse words. Weak decoding can be, and often is, the root cause of comprehension problems. Research has shown that most reading difficulties are the result of unresolved word reading and word recognition difficulties. Inaccurate word reading will manifest itself in comprehension problems. But what if your child reads words accurately and still does not get the gist of the reading material?

Fluency is a factor that is highly correlated to reading comprehension, especially in the elementary grades. Fluency is defined as the ability to read with speed, accuracy, and proper expression. If your child reads accurately, slowly, and labors to sound out every long word, he is not reading fluently and may be expending all his mental energy on word reading and not

51

understanding. An appropriate reading rate is necessary for comprehension to occur, but it should not be at the expense of accuracy. Sometimes, fluency is confused with just reading rate. It is extremely important to see if the reader pays attention to punctuation and uses prosody (the rhythm and sounds of language) and expression when reading.

Weak **Working Memory** seems to be present in many people with learning difficulties. Working memory is the ability to temporarily store and manage information while doing a complex cognitive task. As new information comes in, we need to be able to access information that we already should have and use it to make meaning. For many students, connecting and applying information is a real challenge. Other cognitive skills such as **Processing Speed and Word Retrieval** can impact the ability to understand.

Vocabulary: A Window to Comprehension

Vocabulary cannot be separated from comprehension, and it is the most important factor in developing an understanding of what is heard and read. I will never forget a story my husband shared with me about his coworker's son. The boy must have been about five years old, and he was playing a video game. While watching him play, my husband described a huge opening in the ground as a "pit." The boy, who was not familiar with this usage, insisted that a pit is what you find in fruit. He exclaimed, "It's not a pit; it's a hole!" Shortly after, my husband used "pit" again in the context of it being a hole in the ground, and the child began screaming, "It's not a pit; it's a hole!" We laughed about it, but the child did not find it funny!

Understanding a word in different contexts is crucial to comprehending the meaning of a simple joke. I have seen children laugh seconds after seeing their classmates laugh, realizing that something was funny and they should also laugh just to feel like everyone else. Since vocabulary is highly correlated with reading comprehension, it is imperative to find ways to develop "word consciousness," an awareness of and curiosity about words.

How does vocabulary expand, not just in number of words, but also in multiple meanings? It takes more than repetition to see shades of words; it takes hearing and seeing the word used in different contexts. Conversation and "word talk" help children recognize how to interpret meaning and decipher complex concepts. Giving examples and connecting them to children's own experiences will add meaning and make words memorable. Directly teaching children the multiple meanings of words is also important, but it is not always possible since many words have lots of different definitions. Teachers are in a better position to do this type of direct instruction than parents, yet parents can raise word consciousness in the home and create a language-rich environment, influencing vocabulary growth immensely. Doing crossword puzzles, word jumbles, playing Scrabble, Boggle, and other word games as a family all serve to model word curiosity and foster an appreciation of language. Simply using a dictionary or thesaurus in front of your child models interest in wanting to learn what words mean. It also demonstrates that adults, like children, are learners their whole lives.

The best way to increase one's vocabulary is to read often and widely across multiple domains. When I was in college, my education professors used to say that it doesn't matter what children read, as long as they are reading. This is not entirely true, and research now reveals that it matters greatly what one reads. Vocabulary is limited by opportunities to hear and see words that we would not encounter in our daily conversations. If children only read sports articles and magazines, they will know a lot of technical words related to their interests, but they will be missing out on building their vocabularies through other genres.

For children who struggle to read, it is extremely important for parents or caregivers to continue to read aloud to them often in order to develop their vocabularies. This interaction around words will help children learn double meanings of words and abstract concepts, language that is needed to understand the world. There is a misconception that reading aloud to children should stop when they are old enough to read. There is no substitute for reading books if one is to acquire academic vocabulary. Poor decoding ability should not limit vocabulary development. Getting the joke is really about getting words.

Language Comprehension, including a weak vocabulary, is also aligned with weak reading comprehension. If you have ever heard of the

Matthew Effect, "the rich get richer, and the poor get poorer," this sums up vocabulary development. Vocabulary is accumulated over time, and there is a cumulative advantage to building up a strong word bank from early childhood. The more words we know and understand, the more we will be able to extract meaning from text. **General Background Knowledge** and language skills are also crucial as the material becomes more complex in the upper grades. A fabulous book on the importance of background knowledge is *Why Knowledge Matters: Rescuing Our Children From Failed Educational Theories* by E.D. Hirsch Jr. Following up on his earlier work, *The Knowledge Deficit*, Hirsch makes a convincing argument, based on empirical evidence, that reading comprehension is not a skill that can be taught in isolation. Although it is important for children to be able to summarize, sequence events, infer, compare and contrast, draw conclusions, and self-monitor, teaching and requiring students to practice these skills alone may not be enough without connecting it to background knowledge. Reading comprehension is developed through years of building a base of knowledge, beginning in early childhood. I believe in this theory whole-heartedly and would hope that Hirsch's latest book will prove to educators that teaching comprehension strategies has a limited impact on achievement, especially when students reach high school.

Hirsch believes that "listening ability in early grades is the key to reading ability later on. In listening, the young mind does not have to be slowed down by the new chore of decoding, and so can learn new words and concepts efficiently. Reading aloud to children and classroom discussion should play a big role in the early grades." According to Hirsch, early phonics training should be kept separate from having children listen to and discuss literature and other content-rich subject matter. He emphatically states, "Reading and writing (decoding and encoding) should be taught efficiently, but the knowledge children gain should not be constrained or slowed down by what they are able to decode from the printed word." Phonics alone will not produce improvement in comprehension when grappling with complex texts and topics; however, he states, "… once decoding has been mastered and fluency attained, relevant knowledge becomes the chief component of reading skill." Having background knowledge of a topic allows for a deeper experience, and hence, higher comprehension.

The lack of growth in reading comprehension of high schoolers can be partly attributed to the leveled readers they were given as children in elementary school. Placing children in leveled readers, Hirsch argues, does not give a true depiction of what children can understand. Research by Hirsch and Tim Shanahan, a highly respected professor of literacy and national speaker, has shown that there is no firm scientific basis for using leveled readers to build reading comprehension, develop deep student interest, or make better readers. Practicing fluent and accurate decoding in kindergarten, first, and second grade, while at the same time, trying to grasp the text's meaning, overloads working memory. At that age, exposure to content and vocabulary that is rich and meaningful should be taught through read-alouds, projects, and the arts. Yet, most schools across the country continue to use leveled classroom libraries.

Hirsch also delves into preschool gains and how these gains are lost in elementary school unless there is knowledge-based schooling in these grades. He uses the term, "fadeout," to describe how "vocabulary gain is an incremental process, requiring multiple exposures to a word in multiple contexts, and without reinforcement over time, the word will not get fixed in the mind." Not surprisingly, research shows that children from disadvantaged homes who attended quality early childhood programs do not sustain early progress if their elementary school curriculum is devoid of content. By third grade, those students tend to perform at the same levels as children who did not attend preschool.

Grammar and Syntax, to a lesser degree, are factors that affect reading comprehension. Sometimes, sentences are complex and hard to follow. The reader may lose meaning when trying to figure out how to decipher the message within the structure of the sentence or passage. When combined with a weak vocabulary, a student who has difficulty with this may get lost in a sea of words, making it difficult to answer questions and comprehend.

When being asked about a passage, children need to read the question and clearly know what is being asked. Understanding the question is half the battle. Children frequently become confused by the syntax of a complex sentence or misunderstand what to look for. Furthermore, they must know what information they need to answer the question. Is it a basic, literal question that can be found easily or is it a question that requires inference and judgment based on information that will not be easily found in a passage but can be answered based on a more holistic understanding of the text. Finally, when dealing with multiple choice questions, they should be able to narrow down their choices by eliminating ones that do not make sense. There can be a couple of choices that look right, but there will be a tipping point that can be supported through careful analysis. It would be nice to increase the odds by picking more than one answer, and it is an understandable strategy for children. Unfortunately, the odds of being successful as a student decrease when we cannot support why we choose an answer. These are the skills necessary to read strategically and write convincingly. Information should not be taken at face value; readers and writers need to dig deeper and support what they think and how they respond.

"Close reading" is a popular term used today and mentioned frequently as part of the Common Core State Standards. It demands critical thinking about text, and, especially, thinking about one's own thinking, defined as **Metacognition**. Getting the gist of text is the first step in comprehending, but it is not enough to develop a deep understanding. One must pay close attention to the form, structure, and underlying meaning of a passage in order to thoughtfully support an argument and defend a position. The reader needs to question his own thinking and confirm his patterns of thought using the clues in the text. Many students are impulsive and try to jump to an answer based on a superficial understanding of the text and ignore the important details. Metacognition is a higher level skill that is trainable and necessary for critical thinkers.

Higher level thinking skills, such as **Drawing Inferences**, are difficult for some students. A friend and mentor of mine would use the expression "on the line and off the line" when describing how to locate information. On the line information can be found directly within the passage. Off the line information requires piecing together information that is already there but doesn't directly answer a question. One must formulate a reasonable thought based on clues in the context. Some would call this "reading between the lines"; it takes a little detective work and is much more difficult for the struggling reader.

Finally, some students have **Attentional Difficulties** that interfere with their ability to focus and comprehend what is being read. This is complicated because there could be multiple factors causing the inattention. Many learning difficulties coexist and overlap. Attention Deficit Disorder (ADD) and Auditory Processing Disorder (APD) are perfect examples of problems that present together often, and exacerbate one another. In a later chapter, I will discuss some of the common symptoms of both disabilities.

Without proper diagnosis, a child with reading comprehension difficulties can wind up being treated for the symptoms without the underlying cause ever being addressed.

IS IT A MATH PROBLEM?

I had an interesting conversation with a client regarding her daughter's academic performance. The teacher told her that her daughter reads well, but she struggles in math because she needs the math problems read to her in order to solve them. That did not make any sense. If a student "needs" the math problems read but can understand what to do to solve the problem, clearly the child has difficulty reading the words. This is usually a decoding issue that needs to be addressed through reading instruction and intervention. The child can do the computation and has the mathematical vocabulary and understanding. If the teacher reads the problem and the student still cannot understand the language of the word problem, it is just as likely a vocabulary and language comprehension issue as a math deficiency. Perhaps the student does not understand words that are needed to solve the problem, such as twice, fewer, more than, equation, or parallel. Sometimes, the technical words are understood, but the way the problem is phrased and how the question is asked present difficulties. In either case, the child may have a conceptual understanding and know how to solve it, yet reading is the underlying cause for the "math" problem.

Why is this so confusing? Solving a math problem requires multiple skills. One needs to be able to read accurately, understand key words, interpret what is being asked, access working memory, and be able to plan and solve, which can be a multi-step process. It is not simply a computation question where the child just writes an answer. Figuring out where the breakdown is occurring is the most important part of getting the right help. All other subjects in school depend on reading. If there are decoding and/or language comprehension difficulties, the child will probably struggle in other academic disciplines.

Many subjects in schools are taught in isolation. There are blocks of time for teaching each, and it is usually disconnected from language arts. It would be more effective if children were able to see the connection between word reading, spelling, vocabulary, and math. For example, if children were taught that "fract" or "frag" means to break, they would probably remember the spelling of the words fraction and fragment, understand why fraction and fragment mean part of a whole, and recognize the meaning in a problem. The study and description of how words are formed in language, known as morphology, help with the technical understanding of math and science. Since math and science vocabulary are comprised of Latin and Greek roots, it would be smart to introduce word analysis at the same time as learning concepts. Not only do children enjoy word study, they appreciate when they can recognize patterns and apply this knowledge in their coursework. Many times morphology is overlooked as a way to improve reading comprehension across all subject matter, especially knowledge of words and language in technical subjects.

DEREK – LEARNING WITHOUT BELLS AND WHISTLES

Derek was a sixth grader who was new to the district and, moreover, new to going to school. He was physically abused, recently taken away from his mother and seven siblings, and placed in a foster home. He had only been out of his house to attend church and had no formal education. When I met Derek, he was malnourished and his skin was jaundiced. I was asked to assess his reading and writing skills to see what he knew. I expected very little and assumed the assessment would go quickly. Boy was I wrong. Derek actually read better and understood more than most of the students in Academic Intervention Services (AIS).

Derek might not have been treated well and certainly lacked important skills, but his mother did talk to him, and his siblings spoke to each other. There was a lot of language in his home. I asked Derek how he learned to read. Apparently, his mother had taught him using the bible and educational television. He was not exposed to the outside world and was not aware of many things the average child is involved in today. I was in awe of this child and fascinated by how interested he was in learning. Even though his reading was much more advanced than his writing ability, I knew Derek had the potential to do very well.

This is a stunning example of how children have the capacity to learn without bells and whistles. With just conversation and bible study, Derek assessed above the benchmark for AIS reading. Does this mean every child would be able to thrive despite living in squalor? Absolutely not! But it does reveal that getting back to basics and building language skills, knowledge, and vocabulary can be powerful in our fight against illiteracy.

AUDITORY PROCESSING DISORDER: WHAT?

D o you remember the old SAT questions that included analogies and comparisons to test your ability to recognize relationships between words? Here is one that will help explain the meaning of an Auditory Processing Disorder:

Hear:Noise – Listen:Music

Hearing is a physical and biological activity. One cannot help but to hear noise if his hearing is normal. It takes no effort. Your hearing can be perfect without listening. Listening, on the other hand, requires effort because it is the ability to pay attention to what the sounds mean and to understand them.

Auditory Processing Disorder (APD) is not a hearing loss; it is an auditory deficit that inhibits understanding of auditory information. There are other disorders that can interfere with understanding verbal information, such as Attention Deficit Disorder (ADD), and the two are frequently confused because they can result in very similar symptoms.

People with ADD have trouble focusing and following directions, especially when the information is given verbally and received through just the ears. They may also have trouble remembering information, which is also a symptom of APD. The difference is that people with APD take in the message through normal hearing channels, but a block or a glitch in the nervous system does not allow the message to be processed properly and creates a specific auditory dysfunction. People with ADD do not have a glitch in processing information; it is the attention deficit, not the auditory deficit, which prevents understanding of information. Sometimes, a personal FM Transmitter is recommended for children in classroom situations and allows the teacher's message to go directly to the student's ears through earphones that block out other sounds. Although environmental modifications are helpful, they will not help a child learn how to read, and the child will still need to be taught coping strategies to deal with distractions. Parents are sometimes led to believe that all the learning problems associated with APD will be resolved with the FM Transmitter. This is not the case at all. The at-risk child with APD must receive an effective academic intervention while trying any piece of assistive technology.

The following are common symptoms of Auditory Processing Disorder frequently seen in other disabilities:

• Difficulty understanding verbal information, especially in noisy environments.
• Difficulty following directions.
• Difficulty distinguishing similar sounds in speech – m/n, b/p, d/t/th.
• Difficulty distinguishing similar sounding words.
• Asking for information to be stated again and needing clarification.
• Difficulty with reading and spelling.

Looking at the above list, one can see how a learning disability such as dyslexia, discussed in a previous chapter, can have similar symptoms to APD and ADD. It is not unusual for struggling students to have overlapping learning difficulties that coexist and exacerbate one another. APD, like dyslexia, cannot be cured, but it can be helped through non-medical strategies. ADD, on the other hand, can be treated with medication if considering that option. Whether your child is dealing with APD, ADD, or dyslexia, the frustration of not understanding, or not being understood, can result in behavioral outbursts, or the opposite, withdrawal from participation in activities.

If your child is struggling with reading, spelling, and writing due to an auditory processing problem, it is extremely important to have someone working with your child who is trained in systematically and explicitly teaching the sounds in language connected to the letters that represent them. Multisensory instructional strategies and classroom accommodations can also help ameliorate the difficulties and should be part of an overall plan to support the student.

DEPLORABLE, DEPORTABLE, DYSLEXIA

A witty and cynical political cartoon appeared in Newsday, Long Island on September 26, 2016. The cartoon showed Donald Trump standing at a podium announcing to his supporters, "Half of Hillary's supporters are Deportable," while Hillary Clinton stood at her podium announcing, "Half of Trump's supporters are Deplorable." As I read the cartoon, I shook my head and thought about how these similar sounding words can be a nightmare for someone with dyslexia, a language-based disability. Why? Many people think dyslexia is just reversing letters and not being able to read, but it is so much more. There are a host of tell-tale signs. In the cartoon, the words "deportable" and "deplorable" look similar. The prefixes are the same as well as the suffixes. Only the Latin roots "port" and "plor" are different. Even someone without a learning disability might have to read the cartoon twice to catch the differences and the irony. However, someone who shows signs of dyslexia would either overlook the differences or read these words very slowly to catch the contrasting details, and then might still even miss the meaning. This is not a product of intelligence; people with dyslexia are usually extremely intelligent. Multisyllabic words can be difficult for someone with a language-based disability. Since words like "deplorable" and "deportable" are not in a young child's reading vocabulary, this difficulty might not surface until third or fourth grade. This is why many reading problems are not noticed right away. By middle school, it becomes a real challenge to keep up with reading assignments that require advanced decoding skills.

THE READING SLUMP: WHAT HAPPENS IN FOURTH GRADE?

What happens in the intermediate grades that causes a downward spiral in reading development? For some students, the change is dramatic. In the early grades, such children exhibit few, if any, struggles and appear happy to read. Then, by third grade, it slowly starts to change, and by fourth grade, these same children begin failing subjects that were not problems before. Is it simply the age of the child, the influence of peers, or a lack of interest in books that causes this previously unrecognized problem? It could be, but more than likely it is not pre-adolescence.

An obvious cause is a shift in the type of reading that is expected in fourth grade. Children begin to read to learn, and this type of reading is much more sophisticated on many levels. First, the font size becomes smaller, and the pages are denser with more content. Second, there are fewer pictures. In the earlier grades, some children relied on the pictures as a cueing system that now fails them. Third, they need more extensive background knowledge to understand what they are reading to make connections. Vocabulary is a close cousin of background knowledge, and it becomes increasingly important to know the meanings of words when trying to comprehend a complex passage.

But there is a less apparent cause that seems to be pervasive, yet rarely accounted for. The words have more syllables, and many children have difficulty reading multisyllabic words. There are children who can decode fairly well at the one syllable level but do not know how to read words accurately and fluently when they must read through longer words. Since most decoding instruction stops by second grade at the latest, children are not being directly taught how to read multi-syllable words just at the point when these words begin to become more prevalent. Furthermore, fluency is expected by the intermediate grades and not knowing how to read multi-syllable words negatively affects such children's ability to read smoothly. This is sometimes tricky to detect. Since they can read the shorter words and connector words well, their struggles with multisyllabic word recognition is not noticeable. Some children can read quickly, and some teachers, and even some evaluators, will not recognize a fluency problem. Children will use the context and sometimes even come up with a meaningful substitution for a word. But if they do this often enough, either skipping over words or misreading them, comprehension will be compromised and the downward spiral will continue through the upper grades. Subsequently, spelling and writing will also be affected, as they are more frequently expected to provide written responses in all content areas.

PART III: INTERVENTION

RTI: <u>R</u>EALLY, <u>T</u>HIS <u>I</u>SN'T HAPPENING.......

I remember when the Response to Intervention (RtI) model was first introduced at one of the Regional Coach meetings I attended. It sounded wonderful; instead of waiting for children to fail before recommending them for a special education evaluation, the premise was to catch them early on in their general education classes (which were supposed to be using instruction based on best practices), provide a classroom-based, scientifically research-based intervention, and monitor their results. If the classroom intervention (tier 1) did not show enough progress, the children would eventually be moved to a small group intervention (tier 2) and their progress monitored using a more intensive approach. If this wasn't working, the children would be moved into a tier 3 intervention, which envisioned an even smaller group, possibly more time, or a completely different intervention before a referral to special education was made. As someone who is certified in general education, special education, reading, and administration, I always thought that too many children were being unnecessarily referred to special education, and this model, I hoped, would keep everyone accountable for making sound decisions supported by evidence. Unfortunately, what sounds good in theory and what truly happens in reality are often two different things.

There are too many "ifs" involved in RtI. Let's look at just some of the things I witnessed. First, RtI, as contemplated, is supposed to begin with strong, proven methods at the classroom level, tier 1. RtI also depends on teacher implementation of effective whole class and small group instruction. The classroom teacher is expected to set up an intervention plan for struggling students based on benchmark assessment results given at the beginning of the year. An RtI team, usually a group consisting of a few or all of the following: reading/math specialist, guidance counselor, social worker, psychologist, administrator, and other teachers, helps the teacher decide on a course of action and an agreed-upon plan for each child. The teacher then needs to make the time to work with students who are not making adequate progress, and monitor and document the results. According to the RtI framework, in approximately eight weeks, the teacher and RtI team are supposed to meet again to see if the students are making adequate progress. Can you see how many "ifs" there are already at just this level?

Classroom teachers, already overburdened with a ton of paperwork and responsibilities, were now given even more paperwork and responsibilities. What do you think many of them chose to do? All of a sudden, there weren't any children struggling in their classrooms. Everyone was just fine and dandy. Why should those teachers speak up? RtI just made a lot more work for them. Other teachers would identify children in need of services but would not do the classroom intervention, or if they did, would not document what they were doing. When the RtI team would reconvene to discuss the identified children, some classroom teachers would either be unprepared or come to the meeting with obviously fabricated paperwork, created just to produce "evidence" for the meeting. It would put the RtI team members at odds with some of the teachers. Meanwhile, time was ticking and children were sitting in classrooms without getting the help they needed. The teachers who actually carried out the suggestions and monitored progress were able to move children into a tier 2 intervention with a learning specialist. Yes, this happens in both the best and lowest performing school districts.

But the problems with RtI do not end there. What if there are too many children needing services compared to the number of learning specialists? What if the specialists are not trained in the intervention required for children to make progress? What if "small group" turns out not to be "small" group? What if the pull-out is scheduled during a time when the classroom teacher teaches something new and feels the children cannot miss the work? What if the specialist is not delivering the intervention with fidelity, either by not using the intervention as intended or consistently enough to make a difference? And what if even the specialist isn't assessing and monitoring progress effectively?

As you can see, all these "ifs" complicate the process. A whole year or more can go by without struggling children getting their needs met. It is mandatory that parents know that their children are receiving services, but do they really know what is happening? A recent report dated November 6, 2015 in Education Week entitled, "Study: RTI Practice Falls Short of Promise," reveals how RtI falls short of what it promises to do. It states that the process may hold back some of the children it was originally designed to support. "We're looking at this framework that has developed over the years and how it has really played out in classrooms….We weren't expecting to see this pattern," said Fred Doolittle, the study's co-author.

I am not surprised by the results reported in the above-mentioned study because I was able to witness the shortcomings myself. Parents, however, should have a better understanding of what may be going on. Just because districts promote and package their intervention services with an impressive sounding plan or familiar program name does not mean they are working effectively in practice. This is not to say that every district's RtI process is not working, but it can explain why some parents are baffled by the lack of progress they see in their children.

INTERVENTIONISTS: EXPENSIVE
SUBSTITUTES OR CHEAP ADMINISTRATORS

In addition to the systemic problems with RtI, a number of other impediments result in students not receiving services. It is not unusual for a reading teacher or other school support staff to be pulled to cover a classroom teacher for part of the day or all day when the school cannot find a substitute teacher. There are schools where this happens regularly. In small schools without an assistant principal, and even in larger schools with assistant principals, a specialist will frequently be pulled to do administrative work, such as preparation for state testing, field day organizing, and event planning. This person will be placed in charge of a number of duties that do not fall under his or her job description. Meanwhile, the students needing services are shortchanged.

Another manner in which AIS students miss out on necessary intervention is when the classroom teacher refuses to release students because he or she is doing an "important" lesson, as if to say that reading, math, or other interventions are not important. It is not much better in a "push-in" model where the AIS provider goes into a classroom for a particular purpose but essentially becomes the teacher's assistant because students look at the classroom teacher as the "main" teacher. Such an environment reinforces that the AIS provider is nothing more than a visitor or helper in the room, not an equal. These attitudes are pervasive, and they are reinforced when interventionists and school support staff are asked to act as glorified substitutes during school-wide professional development or other "emergency" situations. What can be done to shift this mindset?

Parents first need to be aware that this is happening in many school districts, some more than others, but I think it happens more often than not. Speak to your children and ask them if they have been regularly receiving their services. Many times parents are under the assumption that once the letter goes out alerting them that their child will receive extra support, it actually happens. This is far from the truth. And school support staff will not always care; some can be part of a culture that accepts what "is" rather than what "should be." Apathy is contagious, and even the children start to recognize this message as a sign that "it just doesn't matter." Parents must be proactive and involved to ensure that their children are getting the necessary help.

Also, parents should be clear on what intervention is being used for their child, what teachers should be working on to remedy their child's problem, and how long it should take to meet a goal. It is nice to be able to say that your child receives a service in school, but do you know what they are actually doing? Do you know why a particular intervention was chosen over another one? Could it be that the provider has been doing something for years and is comfortable doing the same thing, even if it does not address the needs of your child? Besides advocating for your child to receive services, a parent must be knowledgeable about the intervention. Assuming a child is picked up regularly, it is not possible to see progress if the intervention does not target the child's needs.

Try to understand as much as you can about the learning process. If you were shopping for a car, you would do your research about the track record and repair history of your choices. You would not negotiate a deal with a salesperson not knowing the price range, the features you would like to have, and services you would expect from the dealership. Somehow, in education, we blindly trust the professionals to do the right thing. You are your child's first and most important advocate. Even if you hire an advocate, that person can only help you attain the services. It is up to you to understand and support your child's needs to ensure quality, targeted intervention and to keep the school accountable to provide the program and time required to see improvement.

LABELING CHILDREN

You fought with the school district to get services for your child. You may even have hired an advocate to help you. Your child is finally given the label, "Specific Learning Disability." What does this mean? It is actually not very specific at all. Specific Learning Disabilities is defined by the Individuals with Disabilities Act (IDEA) as "a disorder in one or more of the basic learning processes involved in understanding or in using language, spoken or written, that may manifest in significant difficulties affecting the ability to listen, speak, read, write, spell, or do mathematics." It is the largest category of disability with almost half of learning disabled children receiving this label. Dyslexia is included in specific learning disabilities along with dysgraphia and dyscalculia. And each specific one of these specific learning disabilities is not very specific at all. For instance, dyslexia, a language-based reading disorder, can manifest in very different ways with many different underlying problems and overlap with other difficulties.

So with such broad labels, how are they helpful for children needing "specific" interventions to address learning problems? School districts must show that their teams are addressing learning difficulties, but are they, in practice, providing the interventions best suited for children with "specific" skill deficits? Why do we have labels, and fight for labels, if the diagnoses cannot be directly connected to remediation? It's complicated, and I believe the terms are purposely vague to protect the schools from having to offer a "specific" intervention that might require someone with "specific" training, which can add up to an "unspecific" amount of money.

Parents are confused by terminology that is not standard between school districts and neuropsychologists, and this causes more confusion when wanting to know how the learning difficulties will be addressed. A label is no guarantee that your child will get the correct services, which is why it is of utmost importance to understand what your child can do and what he or she cannot do. Parents must ensure that interventions are appropriately matched to specific areas of need and have highly-trained interventionists implementing them correctly. Assessments need to be performed on an ongoing basis, and the results need to be analyzed carefully.

Labels do serve a purpose for many struggling learners and their families who want to identify a problem so they can get the help their children deserve. The school day should be filled with meaningful instruction that works for all children, whether or not school evaluators, psychologists in private practice, or parents can agree on ambiguous terminology. With that said, label or no label, understanding why certain instruction works well, and making sure that children receive what works for their particular needs, should be paramount for optimal learning.

THE PURPOSE OF READING ASSESSMENTS
AND MONITORING

Have you seen the LifeLock commercials on television where a group of masked robbers smash their way into a bank with baseball bats? Everyone drops to the ground in fear except for a security guard who just stands there. The customers in the bank tell him to do something about the robbers, but he explains that he is only there to "monitor" the bank for robberies, not to actually do anything about them. Another LifeLock ad shows a dentist diagnosing a patient with a terrible cavity and then doing nothing. Once again, the dentist just "monitors" the problem. The catch phrase is, "LifeLock doesn't believe in just monitoring problems without fixing them." Now some security guards and dentists might be insulted by the ads, but I think they are brilliant and insightful! We monitor a problem in order to fix it, not merely to "monitor." Unfortunately, in our schools, I have frequently seen reading assessments done regularly on children to "monitor" progress, without any subsequent adjustments being made to address underlying issues.

The purpose of assessments and monitoring progress is to drive instruction, see how effective the instruction has been, and then reflect, diagnose, and either stay the course or change course based on what the information reveals. If assessments were used appropriately, problems would be discovered early and interventions aligned to the actual skill deficits begun promptly. The assessments should be able to point to specific factors that influence performance overall, and subsequent intervention programs should be chosen and used with enough intensity to make a difference. Monitoring is supposed to track change over time so that problems can be addressed, not simply performed for monitoring's sake.

If assessments were truly utilized the way they were designed, we would not see the same students in Academic Intervention Services (AIS) staying in AIS throughout their schooling. Although assessments are necessary to see what the underlying issues are that prevent progress, it is a waste of time if they are not being used to improve instructional choices. Here are some questions that parents should be asking:

- Which skills are lacking or preventing my child from making progress?
- How is the skill deficit being addressed?
- Is my child being given enough time in the intervention to see a difference?
- How many students are in the intervention group?
- Are all the components of the intervention being used with fidelity?

If your child is an "AIS Lifer," it is likely that your child is being "monitored" without the underlying problems being remedied. This is not true intervention.

READING PROGRESS VS. PROFICIENCY

You may hear that your child has gone up a level or two in reading based on a common benchmark assessment. What does this actually mean in terms of your child's skill in learning to read? It might surprise you that your child can show improvement all year and yet still not be reading at a proficient level.

The assessment used in many schools includes books leveled from A to Z and measures reading progress against grade level criteria. The letters, A to Z, representing reading levels from easiest to hardest, are designed to individually assess a child's independent and instructional levels for placement into reading groups. Books for children to choose on their own are also suggested based on these levels so that the children are matched to books they can comfortably read. The assessment consists of oral reading fluency, followed by "comprehension conversations" to gauge understanding. The starting level for each child is based on prior results, and text difficulty is increased until a level of frustration marks the end of the assessment. It can take twenty to thirty minutes to complete the assessment for each child.

Once a reading level is determined, the reading material might be manageable, but it will not necessarily prepare students for more challenging text like that which appears on standardized ELA assessments. Moreover, comprehension conversations can be boring to children and frequently offer little in terms of teaching them how to handle complex reading. Another problem involves how reading levels are chosen. Readability is measured using formulas that do not take into account the influence of the reader's prior knowledge and motivation. Text difficulty actually consists of more than length of words and sentence structure;

background knowledge and motivation can make something more palatable to read and more understandable. Having no knowledge or interest in a subject can make it extremely difficult to comprehend. Keeping children in leveled groups and only exposing them to instructional leveled text can be limiting, as evidenced by the number of children appearing to be making progress and yet not reading proficiently in the upper grades.

Another inherent problem with leveled reading assessments can occur with the administration of the assessment; they are frequently administered incorrectly and produce results that are not accurate. It is not easy to administer lengthy individual assessments and keep the rest of the students in a class doing something productive for thirty minutes. Some teachers lose patience with how long it takes to administer the benchmark assessment and will rush to complete it. Others merely use the levels from the year before and do not bother taking children up to their frustration levels, instead approximating where they think the children should be. Consequently, I have not trusted the reading levels of my students and supplement the assessment with other assessments. As you can see, this leads to more testing which is not very efficient.

Most importantly, a leveled reading assessment does not provide a specific trajectory for students to reach a goal. Since the teacher is observing reading behaviors rather than tracking reading skills, the teacher is left to figure out which underlying skills are causing a child to stagnate. Although the teacher may be aware of the letters representing the actual levels and the desired grade level, just determining a reading level does not pinpoint the skill deficits which need to be addressed. Some students may move up in their reading levels naturally as they progress in the classroom without a teacher doing anything specialized to assist them. Progress, however, does not equate with proficiency, and parents should be asking what the teacher or reading specialist will do to specifically address their child's needs.

READING & SPORTS: PRACTICE MAKES PERMANENT

When I was in junior high school, there was a gym teacher who would remind us during the tennis and volleyball units, "If you can't serve, you can't score." In other words, no matter how well we were able to hit the ball back and forth, ultimately, serving was the key to winning the game. He was trying to encourage us to practice serving, not the whole game, just serving. All great athletes know that repetition is the key to improving, but success at anything requires the right type of practice. Pinpointing an area of concern, practicing a skill correctly, utilizing positive feedback and gentle error correction, while making adjustments along the way, are necessary to produce positive results. Likewise, setting measurable, short-term, achievable goals, and bumping up the goals as they are reached, will ensure one stays on a trajectory for success over the long term.

The same logic applies to reading and writing instruction. Isolated, correct practice will improve overall performance. This does not mean that mistakes are bad; part of true learning is making mistakes. Since "practice makes permanent," it is extremely important to not repeat mistakes again and again. Anything done often enough will become habit, and habits are a lot harder to break than learning to do something correctly from the start. Ideally, if a child does not receive the right instruction when first learning how to read, early intervention would be best. Unfortunately, I have seen children go far too long, repeatedly making the same errors: leaving out small words, skipping over or guessing at difficult words, spelling sight words incorrectly, and using grammatically incorrect phrases without anyone trying to correct or even address these habits. If a student has been exhibiting these error patterns for years, the ingrained habits will be that much more difficult to break. This is why it is necessary for parents and caregivers to understand the reading and writing process and be able to coach their child to reinforce the new learning.

Short, deliberate practice sessions, occurring frequently and intensive enough to create new patterns and make those patterns stick, is critical. In Malcolm Gladwell's book, *Outliers: The Story of Success*, he stresses the importance of deliberate practice over the course of time to master a skill. Focusing on a specific skill, getting it right, and building on a firm foundation allows for steady progress and sustained learning. Children are able to succeed in later sessions when the fundamentals are understood completely. Quality matters, not just quantity. School interventions may or may not be targeted, and time spent in generalized instruction is not efficient. But most importantly, students will never "win the game" if they do not have sufficient, isolated practice opportunities to change the trajectory for learning to read and write. After all, "If you can't serve, you can't score."

NEUROPLASTICITY: YES, THE BRAIN CAN CHANGE

The profiles below highlight brain activity in a dyslexic child before and after an intensive phonics-based intervention. These brain scans clearly show how the language center in the left hemisphere of the brain "lights up" when stimulated with targeted instruction. The bottom scan was done after only two months! It gives hope and reassurance that the brain can change and adapt to its environment.

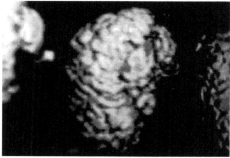

Figure 1 Before Intervention

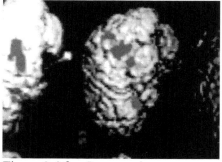

Figure 2 After Intervention

VISUAL DISCRIMINATION

Before the age of eight, some children may confuse letters, numbers, and symbols, such as "d" and "b," or "7" and "1." When this inability to visually discriminate continues beyond the age of eight, it negatively impacts the ability to learn reading, math, and spelling. "Visual discrimination" is the term used to describe the ability to see differences between objects that are similar. When a child is unable to visually discriminate, the child cannot pay attention to subtle differences and may miss important details. There are many activities parents can engage in with their children outside of school to help develop visual discrimination. When I think back to my own childhood, my family worked with me on tasks involving this skill without even knowing they were helping me with academic readiness.

When I was a preschooler, my father used to sit with me and do puzzles. I distinctly remember the chunky, magnetic Disney puzzles. The coffee table was my "desk," and he would lay out the pieces and talk me through the thinking involved and the strategies needed to solve it. When I was easily able to put one together, he challenged me by taking the pieces of two puzzles, mixing them up, and having me think about sorting and solving both puzzles at the same time. This finally ended with five puzzles being the ultimate challenge. As I got older, he showed me how to work on complex jigsaw puzzles without frames. He pointed out the straight edges and showed me how to build the frame first before attempting to match color and shape on the inside.

Another activity we did together was matching socks on the bed after the laundry was done. My father made a game out of it, looking for details and seeing which ones had ribbing or designs that stood out from the rest.

This activity also worked visual memory. If I picked up a sock with a color and design I had seen before, I had to remember which one I had seen and where I had previously placed it.

My mother also taught me to carefully look at details and notice the world around me. We took public transportation everywhere, and I was very aware of how to handle money at a young age. She always gave me coins to pay the bus fare, and I learned the difference between a quarter, dime, and nickel by counting the coins as I threw the fare in the slot at the front of the bus. I remember us sitting together at home by the kitchen table and separating all the coins we had saved, sorting them into piles, and rolling them up to exchange them for bills at the bank.

While my mother was out food shopping, Nana (my grandmother) would play card games with me on the kitchen table and show me how to look for the same suit or number in Rummy. She is the one who taught me to play Old Maid, Go Fish, and War. Another memory I have with Nana is her "penmanship" lessons. She used to have me write repetitive chains of loops and slashes, preparing me to learn cursive writing. These drills are how children used to learn to write, and it also helped me see the differences in letters through proper letter formation.

Unfortunately, many of these organic methods of preparing young children for school and academic success have become relics of the past, as we have become increasingly disconnected from each other while, at the same time, becoming more connected electronically. Although there are computer games and phone apps that work on visual discrimination and memory today, I really believe there is no substitute for the personal connection of someone with a true interest in your well-being, making simple, everyday activities meaningful and educational. As you can see, expensive toys are not necessary to develop academic readiness skills in your child.

LET'S PUT OUR PHONES DOWN AND TALK

On a recent visit to Panera, my husband and I sat near a mother with her young son. She was busy on her cell phone while her son was on his, playing some game that made the most awful, loud noises. She didn't seem to notice or mind because she was engrossed by her phone. Not only was this inconsiderate, it was sad to witness, as there was no conversation or interaction between the two. We decided it would be best to change our seats away from them. From a distance, I kept watching to see if either one would pick their heads up from their devices and acknowledge the other, but it never happened. Unfortunately, this is not a unique occurrence. We all see cell phones and other devices supplanting face-to-face conversations at every turn. This lack of conversation has not only changed how we communicate with one another, it has had a very real, if not indirect, effect on reading comprehension.

Reading comprehension is actually the understanding of language with an added piece of decoding words. People need to be able to infer meaning and make connections, and that is best developed through conversation. Storytelling has been around for centuries, entertaining children with the spoken word and giving them opportunities to visualize a story. With great descriptive language, characters develop, a setting becomes apparent, and events unravel. Children will sit at the edges of their seats waiting for the culmination of a story to see if their predictions are accurate. Not long ago, radio was the vehicle for storytelling, and families would sit together listening to comedies, newscasts, and sporting events, using the spoken words to visualize and piece together stories and information. The family dinner hour was sacred in homes years ago. This was not only a time to break bread, it was a time for families to talk and listen to each other, finding out about school, work, and daily activities.

Talking is the foundation for reading, but today very little conversation happens at home or with friends. Adults need to be mindful that they are modeling behavior for their children. By using their phones instead of encouraging talk, it speaks volumes about what is acceptable in restaurants, at the dinner table, and outside. When a screen entertains us 24/7, there is no reason to learn how to listen or speak. Children especially become used to quick snippets of text talk and videos doing all the visualizing for them. The brain is a muscle, and it needs a workout just like the body. It is not surprising that many children have difficulty with reading endurance. Without practice and exercise, they do not have the attention, focus, vocabulary, and stamina required to read and comprehend deeply for long periods of time.

Critical thinking begins with picking our heads up from our phones, connecting with people, and practicing our language skills. Language comprehension must come before reading comprehension, and reading comprehension can never exceed our language comprehension abilities. Let's put our phones down and talk.

COMPUTER ASSISTED READING INSTRUCTION: DOES IT WORK?

Computer assisted instruction (CAI) has become widespread in schools, but is it being used effectively for struggling students? For some children on the autistic spectrum, it can be extremely helpful; however, according to research, it is an overused and ineffective answer for treating low-performers. I have seen first-hand how computer programs, even the best ones available, become babysitters while the classroom teacher works in groups. The screen tends to hypnotize children as they begin to respond with mindless "clicks" to just answer quick phonics and comprehension questions without really paying attention to what they are doing. Usually, the program has a self-checking mechanism, but children are not engaged enough to think about their errors. Some schools use computerized assessments and get inaccurate results when children with attentional difficulties cannot stay with the task and just "click."

Computerized reading programs can certainly be used to reinforce skills that are taught and provide students opportunities to practice. After all, repetition is needed to reach automaticity of the basics. However, CAI is not nearly as effective in the remediation of reading difficulties as one-to-one tutoring by a highly-skilled professional. Here are some of the reasons why:

• A skilled reading specialist understands how to read the body language of the struggling student. The way the student looks and acts are as important as the way the student sounds when reading.

• A skilled reading specialist will have a deep understanding of all the components of reading, not just one area and not just one program, but a broad base of knowledge and expertise. There is no substitute for this flexibility of instruction.

• A skilled reading specialist knows how to ask the right questions based on what the responses are. A program will be "programmed" to possibly cue the student based on predictable patterns of readers.

• A skilled reading specialist knows how to give feedback based on observable errors in real time. The student will not only recognize errors, the student will know why the mistake was made in the first place.

• A skilled reading specialist teaches students to think about their own thinking (metacognition) when engaged in an activity. Highly effective students use metacognitive strategies. Metacognition reduces apathy and passive reading.

• There are no substitutes for the human voice and physical closeness when working with a student who needs support. The computer program, even with voiced instructions, cannot duplicate the feeling of being with a person who takes an interest.

According to a recent study performed by the Organization for Economic Cooperation and Development, computer-assisted instruction has little or no academic benefit. The results showed children are over-exposed to such programs and computers are overused. "Screens deliver a simulation of individualized instruction. Highly qualified teachers deliver the real thing," reported the OECD. "We should not be automatically throwing out tools that work for unproven ones," said OECD education director, Andreas Schleicher. The study suggests that investing in technology and equipment does not equate with higher levels of performance. Mr. Schleicher makes it clear that access to hi-tech devices does not close the achievement gap. The evidence, rather, supports the moderate use of computers and computer-assisted instruction. In fact, countries with the most advanced technology did significantly worse than countries that were more thoughtful in its use. An article about the study can be read at http://www.bbc.com/news/business-34174796.

INDIVIDUALIZED SUPPORT FOR STRUGGLING STUDENTS

Non-profits such as Reading Partners and Read Alliance use volunteers and high school students to give one-on-one assistance to struggling students in the primary and intermediate grades. Both use a structured approach which provides the reading partner with training, support, and a curriculum that is easy to follow. Both organizations have tracked progress showing improvements in children receiving this extra help. Usually, these types of programs are offered in neighborhoods stricken with poverty and help those who cannot afford private tutoring. Children benefit from having an older and competent helper to guide their reading, listen as they read aloud, and give them feedback. There are so many positives for both the students and the volunteers that it is surprising that more districts, rich and poor, large and small, do not enlist outside help. It is also mind-boggling that school aides and other ancillary school employees, such as hall monitors, who are not on active duty throughout the day, cannot be better utilized for this purpose. Why then, are we not creative enough to encourage retirees, stay-at-home moms and dads, senior citizens, and high school and college students to offer their services in helping young children close the gap before it widens, either as volunteers or for a stipend?

The answer is simple. Teacher unions discourage and block all efforts to bring in outside help in order to protect the interests of their constituents. Their argument is that this type of help can only be given by certified teachers and others are not qualified. In reality, this one-on-one help, guided and monitored by a reading specialist, can be more beneficial than the extra help provided by a teacher, who probably isn't a literacy specialist, working with large groups before or after school. It is usually someone who just wants the extra money, and there is usually no accountability for tracking individual progress. The teacher unions also do not want teacher aides trained to do a job that can be filled by a teacher. In actuality, there are many aides who would love to be a reading partner to a few children throughout the day. Instead, I have seen the aides sit and read their electronic tablets or smart phones while manning a bathroom or exit door. Clearly, schools need people to walk the hallways and oversee the lunchroom and schoolyard, but there is no good reason why they cannot also be helping children. We will sooner put kids in front of a computer for opportunities to practice their reading than enlist humans to engage in conversation and show warmth to a child. We give lip service to upping standards and boosting student performance, but until we are ready to look at options that do not drain taxpayers and cost a fortune to implement, we are hurting children, especially middle class children whose parents cannot afford to hire private tutors and, at the same time, do not qualify for free tutoring.

CHOOSING A PRIVATE TUTOR

As I drive through communities on Long Island or scroll through social media and see the proliferation of tutors and tutoring franchises and agencies, I realize that it must be difficult for parents to make decisions based on what tutors say about themselves. Many will present as experts, but many are "experts" without portfolio. Here are some points to consider when deciding on a reading tutor for your child:

• Experience – There is no substitute for years of practical knowledge and training; however, some educators stop learning and growing after they begin teaching. They teach exactly the same way as when they started. Look for someone who has years of experience and has tested out many teaching methods to determine the best of the best.

• Training – Besides being a licensed teacher, has the tutor engaged in professional development beyond the basic requirements? Teachers are required to continue learning, but have they obtained certifications? Sitting through a presentation is different from actually applying what is taught.

• Programs – Being trained in a program does not qualify someone to be able to know how to teach. Some people say they are using an "Orton-Gillingham" based program, but there are tons of children who do not need or benefit from O-G. As stated previously, programs do not teach children, teachers do. No single approach can address the complex nature of reading difficulties. The prospective tutor should be knowledgeable and experienced beyond O-G. Does the tutor have a range of effective strategies beyond a program? Does the tutor know how to assess children for something other than the one program? The tutor should know how to work with the child rather than the child fitting into the program. Beware of the one-trick pony.

• Generalist vs. Interventionist – A general classroom teacher will have general knowledge about a subject. As an elementary school teacher certified in both common branches (N-6th grade) and special education (K-12th grade), I taught math and science, but I am not a specialist in math and science. From years of teaching, I am confident in my ability to teach those subjects, but there is a tremendous difference between having general knowledge and specialized knowledge and training. Most teaching colleges only require 6 credits in reading, and those introductory courses are broad and theory-based. Even my Master's degree in Reading did not prepare me for what I needed to know in working with the most challenging situations. There is a range of students requiring a thorough knowledge and a variety of effective strategies.

• Certifications and References – Do not feel embarrassed to ask for state certifications, degrees, licenses, program certifications, and references. Tutors should be able to proudly show you credentials and furnish them upon request.

• Cost – Tutoring can be expensive, but you are paying for someone's expertise in a subject. You should know the person who is teaching your child. A name brand company or franchise does not tell you anything about the person who works directly with your child. A high school or college student will be less expensive, but expect there to be a difference. The expression, "Penny-wise, pound foolish," certainly applies. I have fallen into this trap myself on many occasions when looking for piano and guitar teachers for my son when he was a child. There was a huge difference between the people who did this for extra cash and the teachers who dedicated their lives to teaching their instruments.

Explore your options and ask questions until you feel comfortable with your choice.

BLENDED TUTORING MODEL: THE ACADEMIC COACH

Online tutoring services are very appealing for older students and adults needing homework help and subject clarification. But can they work with younger students? There are definitely programs out there that address foundational skills in reading and writing, but there are unforeseen disadvantages to online tutors and computerized programs.

Having an emotional connection and feeling someone cares about what you do cannot be replicated online. Successful tutoring is about forming relationships and trust. Your child should feel a connection with the person and trust that the tutor is giving personalized instruction. We are living in a time when we rely on technology to meet all our needs, but there is no substitute for face-to-face conversation, a warm smile, and an open heart. Studies show that children learn best when their emotional needs are met, and they feel safe in their environment. Your child needs you more than anyone else to help keep him or her on task and practice the necessary skills being taught. Having your child sit by a computer working on reading or writing skills without an adult connecting these skills to reading books or writing essays might not transfer learned skills to generalized usage in the content areas. An app on your phone cannot duplicate the bond between you and your child. In the last few years, Skype and other devices have been used by tutors to "Face Time" their students and give online practice exercises during the week. If a parent oversees these interactions and becomes a partner with the tutor in helping the child, this blended tutoring model can be a successful alternative to the traditional in-person, tutor-tutee session.

Colleges are using a blended learning model more than ever. There are online chats and online tests, and the professors will assign webinars for homework. High school students looking to get extra help regularly go online to sites such as Khan Academy. That might work for a motivated, older student. But for a discouraged, unmotivated, frustrated, younger student, these online tutoring services and computer programs cannot provide the essential component of human connection.

Another option

Parents wanting the expertise of a specialist without the expense of tutoring might want to try coaching. This model gives involved parents and caregivers the support they need and the confidence and strategies to try to help their children on their own. An Academic Coach will provide a starting point based on your child's level, and will provide guidance, feedback, modeling of strategies, and continued assistance to help you, the parent, feel as though you are not going into unchartered territory. The Coach will monitor progress and make suggestions for change depending on individual needs. The coaching model is ideal for families with busy schedules, or who are not able to afford private tutoring, yet need a personalized support system that the schools cannot offer. You also avoid the costly experiments of trying different software, apps, and workbooks that collect dust, similar to a treadmill being used as a coat hanger. The Coach can provide resources for you so that you only purchase what is necessary, not what a salesperson thinks you need.

PART IV:
A COMPREHENSIVE
APPROACH TO LITERACY

SPELLING: A DIRECT CONNECTION TO READING

Why is it necessary to spend time on spelling? After all, we now have spellcheck. Teaching spelling has historically been mostly about testing of words rather than learning how to spell. Many children are discouraged by their results on weekly spelling tests and remain poor spellers. Others do fairly well on the tests, yet spell the words incorrectly shortly thereafter. The rest of the students probably knew how to spell the words already and did not learn anything from studying them. So, do we toss spelling tests and just call them a relic of the past? Well, not exactly. We should not abandon spelling tests altogether, but they should be reevaluated, and teaching how to spell, rather than memorization, should be the focus.

Good spellers are able to see the parts of words and remember the letter combinations that represent the sequential order of sounds within a word. Many children, however, have poor symbol imagery and, thus, have trouble visualizing all the letters in the correct sequence in their minds. Such children resort to memorizing whole words without an understanding of how to analyze a word. Giving a list of random spelling words that have no connection to one another just becomes a memorization task.

Since strong spellers will definitely be able to break a word into its individual sounds, all children should be taught this skill. Segmenting a word is a phonemic awareness skill that some children find easier than others. For example, the word blast has five separate sounds: /b/-/l/-/a/-/s/-/t/. Once each sound can be heard, letters can be mapped to each sound. Successful spellers segment the word, hear it in their minds, and can see the letters and their order in their minds. Poor spellers have difficulty hearing the sounds and visualizing the letters and their sequence. They might spell the word, "blast," as "last," "blat," "dast," "blost," or "blas."

Phonics instruction should be tied to spelling instruction. For example, if a word has a specific pattern, such as "ow" in row and how, children should be taught that the combination of letters can have more than one sound. Likewise, they should also be taught that a sound can have more than one letter combination (ex. the sound /ou/ appears in both how and house).

When words have more than one syllable, children should know how to break the words up into chunks and then match letters to sounds in each part. Reading multi-syllable words can be compared to memorizing a string of numbers - without using hyphens to separate the numbers into chunks, it would be very difficult to remember. Think of phone numbers and social security numbers. It is easier to memorize these numbers when we have visual space between numbers. The same is true for letters, but we cannot break up words with lines or dashes to give us space. We have to learn to do it in our minds using syllables that we hear. For instance, the word, contestant, is a three syllable word. We begin to spell by breaking the word into three chunks, con-test-ant. Each chunk will have letters matched to individual sounds. If a word has a prefix or suffix, children should learn the meaning along with the spelling to help cement it in their minds. Going back to the word, contestant, the suffix –ant means "a person who" (think "accountant" or "occupant"). So the meaning of contestant is a person who enters a contest. Extending this even further, the prefix con- means "with." Putting the parts together, the word contestant literally means a person who joins a competition.

Children should also learn that the vowel in many words doesn't sound exactly the way you would expect. The vowel sound gets swallowed up in the suffix -ant. It is pronounced –int instead of –ant. This is called a schwa. The schwa sound is extremely important to teach to struggling students. When they understand what the schwa means, they will pay careful attention to the vowel and realize it is not enough to simply hear the sounds. Spelling has a visual component. Consider the word "ribbon." When this word is said aloud, the vowel "o" is swallowed up and sounds like a short "i" sound. It is pronounced "ribbin." For spelling, we must remember to see it differently in our mind's eye, and say it in a "perfect recording" voice, "rib-bon." This strategy will help us spell because we are not just relying on what we hear.

Another helpful tip for spelling is to know the origin of the word. For example, the word "chalet" is French; the /sh/ sound will be written with a "ch" and the long /a/ sound at the end of the word is written with "et." "Contestants" in Spelling Bees are always interested in the origins of words, and the popularity of the National Spelling Bee shown on ESPN each year attests to the interest people have in spelling. The sound of the word is not enough to know which phonograms (visual representations of sound) to choose. The origin of words is significant in unlocking the alphabetic code.

Finally, the spelling words should be visualized once the sound, letter combinations, and meaning have been connected. Not all children know how to visualize. Children need to learn how to make a mental picture in their minds. This skill is especially important when learning irregular words (sight words). Children should be able to find the predictable components of a word while concentrating on the irregular part and highlighting it in a way that will help it stay in memory. For example, the word "friend" is often spelled incorrectly, yet, the only tricky letter is the "i". If this letter is highlighted and perhaps made into a picture, the child will focus on remembering its placement in the word (ex. *friend*). If the child is visualizing, he or she will be able to name the third letter and even be able to spell the whole word backwards!

Improvement in spelling will directly improve reading ability by allowing children to read words quickly and confidently. The faster they know the phonograms, the faster they will be able to recognize words. This translates into higher fluency rates, increased vocabulary through knowing word parts and their meanings, and improved writing ability. When students improve their spelling skills, they will be able to focus their writing on content and the message they are seeking to convey.

IS HANDWRITING STILL IMPORTANT?

It seems like everything now is accessible by the touch of a button. Computers, phones, tablets, and just about everything we use has a keyboard. But when it comes to teaching children how to write, should we just teach them to click on the letter? Hold on to your pens and pencils! Research supports the practice of handwriting for its many benefits.

When handwriting is taught while learning letters and sounds, children get the added benefit of a kinesthetic (movement) style to reinforce learning. A multisensory approach uses more than one modality - visual, auditory, kinesthetic, or tactile - to help all learners, especially ones experiencing difficulties. Motor memory helps the body and brain learn together, which is proven to be more effective than relying on the brain alone. Students will also retain the information and be able to retrieve it easier with this type of instruction.

Proper letter formation is another skill that should be automatic, without conscious thought. Writing letters accurately and fluently frees us to focus on the message and how we want to say it, rather than thinking about the mechanics. Some might argue in favor of keyboards and bypassing letter formation, and for some students with dysgraphia, a writing disorder, touch-typing is desirable. For those children, learning how to type with all fingers on the keyboard relieves the pressure of having to write by hand. But for the majority of children, they would be missing out on a very effective form of learning. Handwriting is active, and it engages us more than listening and watching.

A 2014 Princeton University study promotes and supports taking notes by hand as opposed to taking notes on the computer. The researchers found that students who took notes on the computer were not as focused and engaged in the material as their peers taking notes with pen and paper. The reason is simple; we have to be more precise and actively summarizing while notetaking by hand. We can't keep up with the instructor unless we are making decisions along the way as to what is important and what can be left out of our notes. With the computer, students may take more notes, but they tend to type everything and be less engaged, making fewer decisions about what is relevant and what can be consolidated. Frequently, they type mindlessly and even focus on other things. This is not possible when notes are taken by hand.

It seems like we have to be more proactive to create opportunities for gross and fine motor movements in the digital age. It is very easy to leave kids looking at screens and sitting inside, passively learning through television shows and the computer. The research on handwriting, I believe, should shape our thinking about what children need today. Attention should be given to handwriting as another channel for learning how to read, spell, and write in early childhood. To that end, educational standards should be reassessed to include explicit handwriting and notetaking by hand.

ESSAY WRITING: A STRUCTURED APPROACH

Why do some people reach their goals and others do not? Many people are under the assumption that willpower is necessary to achieve what we want. On the contrary, willpower often creates stress and causes us to focus on what we cannot or should not do. It is much better to focus on what we can do and begin by making behavioral changes that include preparing and planning. Successful goals should be broken down into simple, doable action steps that can be monitored easily. It is important to stick to the plan faithfully at the beginning until new habits and ideas are incorporated into our lives.

When students sit down to write an essay, I have noticed that the struggling writers are the ones least likely to have a structured plan and are most resistant to the process; they just want to bypass the planning stage and get to a final product.   Unfortunately, failing to prepare is preparing to fail. Sitting with pen in hand and blank paper for lengthy amounts of time will not make ideas just pop into your head. Writing requires detailed planning which can best be learned with coaching and support.

Compare writing an essay to a diet plan. Both can seem painful and overwhelming, and most people think a diet is about what they can't do or shouldn't do. Negative thinking and willpower won't work over the long haul. Making small behavioral changes will work because feelings of punishment and deprivation are removed. For instance, there is a diet called the 21 Day Extreme that uses pre-measured containers for all the different food groups and offers choices of what you can eat for each one. If one follows the tightly controlled plan, the choices are there for you without too much thinking. It is easy to prepare for a successful day of eating when everything is structured to help you reach a goal. If one sticks to the plan for a set number of days, healthy, portion-controlled eating becomes much easier and a new habit is formed. In addition, encouragement and guidance given by a caring coach can make the difference; such coaching and support groups have been the key for many dieters attending Weight Watchers. This is the same mindset required for successfully writing an essay; a structured format practiced repeatedly will become automatic, especially if there is someone giving positive feedback and direction. Once the structure is in place, this strict regimen can become flexible. Writing, like eating, can and should be a pleasurable experience.

Getting started is the most difficult part of writing. For struggling students, writing is intimidating. Most writing programs have similar components that follow the different stages of writing, and there are many structured programs that can help students improve and gain confidence. I have found the following process helpful:

Students should be encouraged to brainstorm ideas without inhibition. They should just write down whatever comes to mind. The writing process begins with generating ideas around a topic, and once they can see their ideas on paper, it will be easier to choose an interesting topic. Adults can help by prompting children through conversation. Talking out loud to help children clarify their thinking supports writing. The chosen topic should be placed in the middle of a page, and then they should again try to freely write down ideas around the topic.

Next, students should group the ideas they jotted down together to create at least three main points with headings and supporting details. The brainstorm should now be transferred to an outline for planning. A menu of transition words and phrases, such as "First," "However," "Therefore," "Next," "In addition," and "As a result," will help them feel confident in expressing their thoughts in paragraphs. Different types of writing require different transitions for sequence, comparison, or "cause and effect" and need specific words to let the reader know the text structure.

The outline is the key to taking scattered ideas and putting them into a logical, linear format. Then, paragraphs can be formed using a topic sentence, main ideas, supporting details, and a concluding sentence. Writing the first draft should be easier having an outline for reference.

With a checklist to review spelling, punctuation, and sentence structure, students will then be able to revise and edit their work. Finally, they should be looking at their work from the point of view of the reader to see if it is easily understandable. Clarity should always be the main objective.

Part V: The ABC's before the ABC's

READING ABILITY AND SELF-ESTEEM

The concept of self is formed in the early years, and for children reading ability is highly correlated with self-esteem. Learning to read can be a source of pride for a young child as well as a source of embarrassment. Struggling readers feel as though everyone in the class is staring and laughing at their mispronunciations of words, even if this isn't happening. They become so self-conscious and sensitive that school quickly becomes an unhappy place. If this sounds like your child, it is important to be aware of what is happening and take steps to intervene.

Reading aloud can be a devastating experience for struggling readers. Some teachers ask children to participate in what is called round-robin reading which entails taking turns reading aloud. Round robin is not effective for anyone; the struggling reader spends time trying to anticipate the moment he or she will be called on and misses the meaning of what is being read by others. When the struggling reader is asked to read, the other children quickly become impatient; some raise their hands while the child is reading, others roll their eyes and sigh, and some do snicker. Parents should question this practice and speak to the teacher about the negative consequences. Although teachers do need to listen to children read aloud for progress monitoring, error correction, and assessment, reading aloud can be accomplished during small group work or an independent reading conference, without traumatizing the child.

Parents should try to create an inviting environment for reading at home. Books should be connected to warm, upbeat experiences, and children should be encouraged to explore their interests through books and other reading materials. Struggling readers generally become disenchanted with reading and avoid books at all costs, so high interest books give them a reason to keep reading, even when motivation is low. Since such children already have negative feelings attached to books and reading, reading should not be used as a punishment. I know some parents will add extra time or extra pages as a way to discipline children, but reading should never be used for this purpose.

Reminding children that reading is not tied to being "bad" or "good" is an important message. We must be very careful with our words, and children should not be labeled with language that lowers expectations. Negative words may become self-fulfilling prophecies, as many people tend to believe what they hear when it is said often enough. When I was taking an online course, we were asked to read a book called *Courageous Learners*, a book about children struggling with learning challenges. I loved this title and the thought that went into choosing language that positively depicts a challenge. Imagine if all struggling students saw themselves as courageous? This is much different from telling children they are wonderful, amazing, and smart. Many children feeling badly about themselves will not believe this and think those words are untruthful. A better way of complimenting children is to compliment the effort and be specific about what improved. "You really put a lot of effort into this book report and gave great details about the main character" is an example that specifies what the child did rather than what you think of the child. If we want to build self-esteem, we must realize that words are powerful and children will respond according to how we speak to them.

A WINNING ATTITUDE FOR READING SUCCESS

Competitive athletes have it. Glamorous movie stars have it. Successful business people have it. It's called a Winning Attitude. Nobody has ever succeeded in their chosen profession without first thinking they could succeed. They visualize themselves doing exactly what they want with great detail. They can hear compliments and applause, see the touchdown, hold the trophy, and feel the thrill of victory. This all occurs before it actually happens. The mind is a doorway that leads to the reality of achieving our goals. It is very easy to point out those among us with winning attitudes, as well as those of us who are stuck in a distressed mindset. Struggling students fall into the latter group, and it is this defeatist attitude that affects performance.

Let's take a closer look at this vicious cycle. A struggling student might have difficulty keeping up in class, falling behind in assignments, not understanding the directions, feeling embarrassed when called upon to answer a question, and generally not feeling comfortable or happy in school. Such a student might be accused of not working hard enough, or might be given a label such as "lazy" or "unmotivated." Meanwhile, the student is actually trying with all his might to be a strong student, only to be reminded again and again that his efforts are not worth it. So, the message, "Why bother?" is now shaping his reality. He becomes easily distracted, shows disinterest, and is blamed by others for his failures. Does this remind you of your child? Does this remind you of yourself? Perhaps you have tried to lose weight, begin exercising, or get organized. Without being able to see a successful outcome, did you become quickly discouraged and give up?

When students are not paying attention, it is hard to distinguish which came first, the negative attitude or the lack of focus. If there are underlying learning difficulties, which make everything harder and take longer to accomplish, the students will have a hard time putting forth the effort to keep trying. Students who can maintain a positive attitude and stay single-focused, or learn to do so, become strong students. This becomes a self-fulfilling prophecy because they can actually visualize success. They "see" a reason to work toward a goal and can apply themselves. Without a positive attitude and laser-like focus, the prerequisite skills for learning anything, failure is imminent. As the saying goes, "What we resist persists," and when our hearts and minds are not aligned with our goals, it is very difficult to move into a true learning state. Students feel the flow of learning when they have confidence and can see the connection between hard work and results.

INTENTION AND AWARENESS: RETURN ON INVESTMENT

We all need to be mindful of what we do and why we do it when working with our most precious assets - our children. It is indisputable that spending time each day reading to children has a cumulative effect, increasing vocabularies and oral language skills. By making an effort to be involved in our children's lives, demonstrating a commitment to their health and well-being, reading to them, and building relationships, it is expected that this investment will yield strong returns. According to a financial dictionary, Return on Investment (ROI) means to measure the gain or loss generated on an investment relative to the amount of money invested. This definition of thinking about our gains and losses compared to our investment, whether an investment of time, effort, or money, should be thought about in all that we do. For instance, just as reading daily to our children reaps dividends, on a more global level, investing in early childhood education (spending money on quality childcare, early literacy, and parent education) has been proven to generate a strong ROI. Therefore, every investment requires thought and planning to weigh the benefits, losses, and anticipated outcomes. Once a decision is made to commit to something new, a diet, a sport, a reading program, growth only occurs if taken in small increments, done often, and with focused intention and awareness. This last point is usually the element of change that is overlooked and underemphasized.

The power of consciously thinking about what we do and why we do it can make the difference in seeing our goals realized. If we stop, breathe, and think about what we are doing in the moment, we can keep working toward the desired outcome. Let's look at some examples of how clear intention and awareness work. When learning to drive a car, the new, inexperienced driver is aware of every step. It takes getting behind the wheel often and practicing the steps with great concentration until, one day, the driver is no longer thinking about every move. It requires being familiar with the car and driving on familiar roads before one can gain the confidence to drive on unknown roads and travel with ease. We often don't realize how much effort it takes at the beginning, yet the desire to drive is so strong, the new driver keeps getting behind the wheel, trusting that there will come a time when all these individual steps will blend together and be automatic.

If you have ever witnessed tai chi performed in the park, this is another example of how the mind must be engaged to progress. A tai chi practice involves very small conscious movements practiced often over years. It looks like a fluid, weightless dance that is performed easily, but those moves are actually a series of specific steps that have been learned, practiced slowly, consciously, and with great concentration. The experienced practitioner goes through the basics of tai chi automatically and builds on this foundation. One can see how it takes more than a small change, effort, and time; it takes intention, awareness, and desire to maximize an investment.

THE VALUE OF PLAY

According to an article appearing in Newsday, Long Island, entitled, "More Time for Play," the Patchogue-Medford School District extended recess by twenty minutes in order to educate the "whole child." Some would argue that this is a waste of time; others might say that recess and gym can be eliminated altogether. Since Common Core has been implemented and there is a push for higher standards in our schools, doesn't this change in the district's schedule contradict everything that we hear? It does, but contrary to popular thought, movement is not a nicety that should be looked at as a reward for children. The connection between body movement and brain activity is powerful, and both children and adults need to physically move to keep the learning channels open and active. A lazy body is a lazy mind. More districts should be following the mind, brain, and education studies which clearly show that the brain develops like a muscle and requires challenging exercises as well as rest to allow for it to strengthen. Taking a "brain break" by moving or meditating helps the brain function better. If children are chronically stressed, they will struggle with memory, recall, concentration, and overall general cognitive skills. Training the brain to function at optimal levels of performance requires time to absorb information and process it. This is why a combination of physical exercise and sleep are important for a healthy brain.

The Pat-Med School District should be commended for trying to make a change that responds to children's needs rather than the adults looking from the outside in. This initiative, however, would be even more productive if the twenty minutes were broken up into smaller increments and spread throughout the day. The latest research states that we should work with concentrated effort, single-focused, with no multi-tasking, for twenty-five minutes, and then get up and take a break for five minutes.

This is called the Pomodoro Technique, and much has been written about the benefits of rotating work with brief rest periods. Exercise and conscious breathing, such as mindfulness meditation, stimulate hormones to help the brain work effectively.

Pat-Med is progressive, and almost defiant, in their disdain for the Common Core by showing other districts that they are sick of all the demands being placed on teachers, parents, and students. Let's see if other districts follow suit. Certainly, we have seen the negative effects of reducing or eliminating recess, gym, and the arts in our schools, and pushing children beyond their capabilities. It just does not improve academic outcomes.

IMPROVING MEMORY

So much information is accessible through the internet today, yet we forget most of what we see and hear. Why? Because we only remember what is significant to us.

Think of what you remember in your life. I will never forget Sept.11, 2001. I was a first grade teacher at the time, and school had just begun a couple of days prior to that fateful day. I was getting ready to do our Morning Meeting routine and the principal, who happened to be a first year principal at the time, came into my room asking if I had any relatives working at the World Trade Center. I couldn't recall knowing anyone who worked there but was puzzled by the question. She whispered that one of the buildings was hit by a plane and it could be an act of terrorism. She was going around the school, room by room, alerting the staff and letting us know that some parents might be picking their children up early. By the end of the day, I had only half my class with me, and all I could do was wonder how my own children (one was in fourth grade and the other the same age as my students) were doing. Finally, I got in my car and turned on the radio to see what was happening in the world. It didn't sound real to me; I felt like it was a Batman movie and "Chaos" had hit "Gotham City." When I finally reached my street, I saw a lineup of cars parked by my house. My heart was in my mouth, and I could not catch my breath. What was happening? I quickly found out that my wonderful neighbor and dear friend worked for Cantor Fitzgerald in the Twin Towers. Somehow, it never came up in conversation; I just knew he worked as a broker on Wall Street. For days, we were calling hospitals trying to find out information. He never returned that day, and I will remember it for the rest of my life like it happened yesterday. But the funny thing is, ask me what I did yesterday, and I can barely remember.

Significant events have meaning, and we remember meaningful events. Whether the event is joyful, frightening, sad, hurtful, or surprising, we will remember something when there is an emotional response. In school, most children are not moved by what they see or hear. They can physically see with their eyes and hear with their ears, but, frequently, they don't find the information significant to their lives. They will remember the hurtful comments of other children, and they will remember the lunch table clique laughing and pointing. But "area equals length times width, A=lw," just doesn't have the same significance.

How can we use this information as parents and teachers? First, we should try to attach a reason to what we are teaching that resonates with our children. We might think everything we say and do is important, but our children might not feel the same way at the moment. Give them a good reason that motivates them, and there will be a better chance of the information being stored. For example, if my child likes to bake, reading the directions and knowing fractions would be important. Secondly, try to make an emotional and personal connection with the information. Through storytelling, help your children find their own "stories" to bridge what they hear and see with what they choose to remember. Everyone has a different capacity to remember, and some people are better equipped than others. Everyone can make a choice to remember more if they use a multisensory approach. Engage as many sensory cues as possible to help them visualize the experience. My artistic daughter always used visuals and hands-on activities like cooking to remember math concepts. The positive feelings she had while creating a dish cemented facts that she found difficult to memorize. This combination of setting a clear, meaningful purpose, making it personal and emotionally charged, and visualizing will add significance and help their brains function at full capacity.

MESSY THINKING

Doesn't it seem as though parents and children can look at a messy room and see the same thing differently? In my mind, I am thinking to myself, "Why does this have to sit on the floor? Doesn't it bother you? How long does it take to just put it away or throw the clothes in the hamper?" In the meantime, my son or daughter is probably thinking, "What difference does it make? Why doesn't she leave me alone?" If your child has a messy room yet is very organized for school and accomplishes all assignments, there probably is no need to be concerned. You might like every room in the house to be tidy, but it can quickly become a power struggle and might not be worth fighting over. However, if the messy room is indicative of "messy thinking" and other issues involving organization, time management, and planning, it might be a sign of an overall problem with what is called executive functioning skills. Remembering information, prioritizing tasks, beginning an assignment, and handing in homework on time can be challenging. Many children do not know where or how to begin to clean. The parent expects it to be done but doesn't explicitly show the child how to get organized. If there are executive functioning issues, the child really needs the task to be broken down into manageable steps. Don't assume your child knows or can do it without demonstrating exactly what you mean when you say, "clean your room." Make a list of each task and "think aloud" as you show your child how to do it. If you tell him that each item must go back in the same place after using something, and everything should be put back by the end of the day, he will learn to maintain his space and know what to do. Again, a messy room without other difficulties is nothing more than a messy room. For more information on learning and attention issues, visit the website, www.understood.org.

THE MOST INEFFECTIVE STUDY STRATEGIES

Parents might be surprised to learn that rereading the textbook and looking over one's notes are not effective study strategies. Many of you are probably thinking, "I would be thrilled if my child reread books and reviewed notes." It seems hard to understand, but the brain does not absorb information that way. Students become frustrated because they really believe they have studied and can't understand why their grades don't reflect their effort. Parents don't believe them because the test results are weak. How can this be?

First, many students superficially go over the words in a book or their notes without actively learning the material. It is not enough to open the book; the student needs to actively try to understand the content.

Secondly, many students highlight too much information. They are not being selective in the process. These students mindlessly pick out what they think should be remembered. Again, they may think they are studying, but they are not actively involved in learning and retaining the information for retrieval at a later date.

Third, and most importantly, many students have never been taught how to study. Usually, teachers will assign a chapter or two and tell students they will be tested on the material the next week. The teacher's expectation is that students will take responsibility and do what is required to prepare. Unfortunately, many students simply do not know how. Furthermore, many teachers will tell them to "review" their notes to study for a test. Such teachers might, themselves, be under the impression that this is the best way to study.

Finally, students frequently have more than one subject to study at a time, and they are not fully committed to any one task. By looking over their notes, they trick themselves into thinking that they are putting in the effort. As discussed in an earlier chapter, deliberate practice, just like effective studying, requires more than just investing time. They are not using their brains efficiently to learn. The brain is not a storage container; the more information that is thrown in, the more one needs a brain-based strategy such as brief but focused practice sessions, summarizing notes daily, and the use of rhyme, acronyms, and novelty to make it stick.

Students with poor study habits usually do not judge time correctly, do not prioritize, study while multitasking, and do not put in the hard work it takes to truly know the material.

To begin, students need to focus on one subject at a time. They should get into the habit of making checklists to see what they need to do and give each task a certain amount of time. Not only will a checklist keep the students on task, it also provides a great sense of accomplishment as each item is checked off.

In order to gauge the time necessary for each task, students need to prioritize each item on the list to make sure they are focusing on the right things. They should be aware of all due dates and see how much time is required to actively learn the material. Next, they should decide on the three most important tasks and judge the time it will take. Those are the items they need to focus on first and foremost.

Finally, they need to remove all other distractions, including the biggest distractor of all, the cell phone.

How can parents help? A true test of deep understanding is to be able to teach the material to someone else. Allow your child to teach the material to you. Ask questions and have him or her clarify the information. Encourage spaced practice and thinking aloud about the subject. Discourage cramming for tests, which might work in the moment, but does not work for long term retention and retrieval. Ultimately, successful studying is about being actively engaged and setting up proper time management strategies.

ALTERNATIVE TREATMENTS FOR READING AND WRITING DIFFICULTIES

Essential oils, nutritional counseling, mindfulness and meditation, yoga, Brain Gym and energy medicine, computer games and challenges, positivity, vision therapy and colored overlays, and even chiropractic manipulation and massage have been explored in the treatment of learning difficulties and disabilities. There is much research on the mind and body connection that clearly shows that academics are affected by more than intelligence, and the brain can be developed and changed with targeted, repetitive interventions. It would make sense to assume that alternative therapies such as the ones mentioned above would be able to alter patterns in the brain, yet there is nothing conclusive in the research that affirmatively supports their use. Although I believe in using scientific, research-based strategies with proven results, I am not opposed to the use of alternative treatments as a supplement to instructional remediation.

Eating well and avoiding sugar in one's diet seems to be a logical first step. Real food as opposed to packaged, processed food with preservatives is important for all students, not just ones with learning difficulties. Drinking plenty of water, while avoiding sweetened drinks, keeps the body and brain hydrated for thinking clearly. Recently, "healthy fat," such as that found in avocados and olive oil, has been found to support healthy brain activity. Fish oil supplements, in particular, have been found to have important benefits that are being explored for children as well as adults for memory and brain functioning. I encourage all families to learn about food as medicine before jumping to pills to enhance concentration.

Aerobic exercise impacts brain activity and focus. Promoting movement in children for better learning outcomes, and making recess and physical education mandatory in school should be encouraged. Sitting too much throughout the day is unhealthy for the body, and it is not beneficial for learning. Specific exercises that cross the midline of the body have been found to also help children with learning disabilities. It is worth noting that this type of "energy medicine" is being tried for all types of physical and emotional problems, and scientists are recognizing its value more than ever.

Years ago, yoga and meditation were thought to be "New Age," used only by hippies and oddballs. Now their advantages are well documented. Stress reduction techniques such as mindfulness have been slowly becoming daily practices in some progressive schools as more and more research supports learning ways to calm oneself and practice self-control. Increasing focus and learning to ignore distractions affect reading comprehension since reading requires an active mind to make meaningful connections.

The sense of smell can be engaged in working with struggling learners. Rosemary, an essential oil, has been shown to have multiple health benefits and boost learning and memory. Other essential oils such as peppermint can wake up the brain; lemon can help with focus; and lavender can relax us before bedtime. Although essential oil use seems to be experimental, professionals have been trying these alternative therapies more than ever.

Vision therapy used by some optometrists has been controversial, yet I have had clients who state they feel more comfortable and relaxed reading after treatment. They also feel that the colored plastic overlays they put over a page of print cut glare and allow their eyes to focus better.

I believe in holistic medicine and would never discourage anyone from trying alternative therapies to optimize learning; however, it is not a substitute for language-based reading and writing instruction. Children still need to learn how to decode print, spell words, comprehend text, and write coherently. There are no magic pills that can quickly cure a reading and writing disability, and I would cautiously read up on all treatments before spending my hard-earned money. The science surrounding Mind, Brain, and Education is a growing field. It is important to not rule out complementary treatments.

Part VI: af-FLUENT™ Learning for All

When so many children are not succeeding, the most important factor is a faulty curriculum. We must begin to fix the problem by taking a stand. By ignoring the real problem and focusing on factors that are difficult to control, such as societal issues and economic status, we continue to make excuses for failure. A Band-Aid will not work on a gaping wound. Giving all children the right tools from the start and making the decision to put children before the needs of the adults will change the outcome. If we continue to recycle inefficient strategies and blame the victims, we will continue to have poor results. We must protect children against the "experts" trying to sell programs, education gurus wanting us to buy into theories that do not work in the real world, and unions putting their constituents before children. We must protect children against biased evaluators, universities with their own agendas, and leadership that perpetuates a myth that the problems are about money. We can't keep throwing money at a problem when it is really about mindset. Affluent learning begins with an af-FLUENT mindset. The following plan summarizes the components of a learning framework that I believe works for all types of learning, regardless of subject, age of the learner, or discipline:

• **Attitude** – What does this look like? Positivity is contagious and learners need to feel that they are supported by people who believe in their ability to accomplish a task. Human beings tend to focus on the negative, perceiving the worst in what they hear and see. Learners are doomed from the start if they don't believe that success is possible. Any successful person will tell you he first visualized success and "saw" a winning outcome. Positivity does not come naturally for many people, but it can be taught. Through modeling and explicit training, a person can learn to be a positive thinker, setting the stage for all learning.

Neuro-linguistic programming, better known as NLP, involves the three components that affect how we view a situation - neurology, language, and programming. The mind listens to the language we use, and the connection between the two shapes our reality. If we engage in negative talk often enough, we "program" that repetitive message into our belief system, making it difficult to see ourselves as winners. By changing our language and being aware of how words matter, we can reprogram the messages we feed our minds. Children are mirrors of their environment, and change begins with changing ourselves. By the age of six years old, the subconscious mind has downloaded messages from the environment to create the concept of self. The picture can be changed with messages of positivity and changing one's beliefs.

• **Focus** – What does this look like? Without developing the skill of paying attention, very little can be accomplished. Like attitude, this skill can be developed and taught. Some people will brush this aside and jump to pills before trying other methods. I believe that mindfulness practice can assist learners of all ages and should be incorporated into the learning process. The ability to calm oneself, ignore distractions, and concentrate is necessary for productive studying of any subject or discipline. Research supports a mindfulness practice for more than stress reduction, and many schools across the country are encouraging staff to use mindfulness techniques in classrooms today. I received training in mindfulness through a program offered by Mindful Schools. The curriculum was practical and easy to implement. The actress Goldie Hawn also began a mindfulness foundation and wrote a book entitled, *Ten Mindful Minutes*. This book stirred my interest in mindfulness for children and how it can be helpful in schools. The point really is that we are more in control of ourselves than we realize, and we can access this control if we know how. Other methods, such as brain training through targeted movement and exercises that specifically cross the midline of the body, yoga, martial arts, and dietary changes, can also sharpen focus.

Together, attitude and focus underscore all learning, and we need to help learners develop both BEFORE we can expect learning to be successful.

• **Facts and Foundational Skills** – What does this look like? This book has discussed the importance of a phonics-first approach to reading instruction and how no comprehension skill taught will work for children who are not able to read words. Whether it is reading, writing, math, science, playing a musical instrument, or learning to drive a car, we all need the basics. Foundational gaps will always catch up to us at some point and hold us back, forcing us to relearn and retrain our brains. Many do not ever fill in those gaps and continue to struggle, not appreciating or understanding the importance of knowing the basics accurately and automatically. I remember learning this hard lesson when we hired a different piano teacher for our son. The new teacher was a stickler for proper hand alignment because it was important to keep the wrists up when playing complicated, classical pieces. The first teacher did not encourage hand alignment because the pieces were contemporary and simple. My son had to retrain his mind and body, which is much harder than learning the correct way in the first place.

• **Language** – What does this look like? Understanding important technical vocabulary connected to background knowledge facilitates new learning and must be developed while learning the facts. The more we know about a subject, the better we can comprehend. Precise words and shades of language help us file new information into its proper place. Making connections is dependent upon communicating our thoughts using words and ideas that have developed over time. Language comprehension involves a body of knowledge and broad vocabulary that build the foundation for further learning and skill acquisition. Textbooks in advanced courses assume that students have the vocabulary and language to understand the material. The books would be twice the size if they had to explain every concept and word that might not be understood. Newspapers assume that the reader has a base of knowledge to understand the articles. We can never fully understand a subject without possessing the crucial skills and language necessary for deep understanding.

• **Use It or Lose It** – What does this look like? Repetition, targeted practice, repetition, feedback, repetition, error correction, repetition, repetition, and repetition building to automaticity will ensure that the basics are mastered. Some learners need more practice and more opportunities to practice, and using information with cyclical practice moves learning from short term memory into long term memory, making information available to us when needed to perform multi-step tasks. When we overlearn the basics, we free up space in working memory, which allows us to learn more complicated information, develop critical thinking skills and reach unconscious competence as discussed in a prior chapter.

• **Engagement** – What does this look like? It is difficult for us to learn something new without being an active learner. Multisensory strategies engage more than one way to input information through visual, auditory, and kinesthetic channels. "Mind maps," better known as graphic organizers, help us to see our thinking in a logical way and make connections through charts and symbols. Color-coding important information signals the brain to remember in a way that allows us to access what we need at a later time. Memory strategies such as making up rhymes, acrostics, songs, and movements help us connect information so that we do not forget it. I am sure most of you have used any number of the above strategies and can still remember the cueing strategy associated with learning the information. I still think of ROY G. BIV when I want to remember the colors of the rainbow. I still think of HOMES when identifying the Great Lakes. Engagement can look different for each person, and it will be different depending on our preferences. Learners should know that passive studying doesn't work as well as actively participating in the learning process. We need to tell children that growth in any area of our lives takes work and determination. One does not grow watching others do the work.

• **Nail the Important Ideas** – What does this look like? Learning involves making decisions about what stays and what goes. It can be compared to cleaning out your closet and deciding what you wear often and what is just taking up space. When your dresser drawers hold just what you need in an organized way, you can easily find the clothing. Clutter prevents us from accessing what we need when we need it. Our minds are like closets and dresser drawers; if we don't make decisions about what is important, we will be filled with useless information that interferes with remembering what is necessary. Training students to think about their own thinking, and having them question themselves regularly about what should stay and what can be ignored is actually a life skill. Making decisions about who is important to you and stays in your life, while limiting or avoiding contact with people who give you more grief than satisfaction is very important when trying to plan your time efficiently. Paring down helps summarize what we need to be successful.

• **Talk, Test Yourself, and Teach It to Others** – What does this look like? Very simply, when we know and understand a subject or domain of knowledge, we can discuss it easily and teach it to others. If we quiz ourselves or have family members or friends ask us questions, we should be able to respond thoughtfully. The ability to express what we know confidently and fluidly is a true test of internalizing information deeply. When this is realized, a learner can be expected to transfer new learning to other content areas and situations where this information would be useful.

One definition of "**affluent**" means having a great deal of money. I choose the definition meaning "**flowing freely and in great quantity**" to describe what learning should be. Whether it is learning to read or something else, we are affluent when we have learning opportunities that make sense, coming to us happily and easily, through explicit teaching strategies.

REFERENCES

Archer, A. (2010) Explicit Instruction: Effective and Efficient Teaching. New York, NY: Guilford Press.

Gladwell, M. (2011) Outliers: The Story of Success. Boston, MA: Back Bay Books.

Hawn, G. (2011) Ten Mindful Minutes. New York, NY: Penguin.

Hirsch, E.D. (2016) Why Knowledge Matters: Rescuing Our Children From Failed Educational Theories. Cambridge, MA: Harvard Education Press.

Hirsch, E.D. (2006) The Knowledge Deficit. New York, NY: Houghton Mifflin.

McGuinness, D. (1999) Why Our Children Can't Read and What We Can Do About It: A Scientific Revolution In Reading. New York, NY: Touchstone.

Wilson, D. (2010) Courageous Learners: Increasing Student Achievement. Orlando, FL: BrainSMART.

ABOUT THE AUTHOR

Faith Borkowsky, Owner of High Five Literacy and Academic Coaching, is a reading and literacy specialist with thirty years of experience as a Classroom Teacher, Reading/Learning Specialist, Regional Literacy Coach, Administrator, and Private Tutor. Faith is Orton-Gillingham trained and is a Wilson Certified Dyslexia Practitioner listed on the International Dyslexia Association's Provider Directory.

Faith has extensive training and experience in a number of research-based, peer-reviewed programs that have produced positive gains for students with dyslexia, auditory processing disorder, ADD/ADHD, and a host of learning difficulties. New York State certified in Elementary Education, Special Education, and Reading, Faith stays current, is always learning, and continually attends professional development in brain-based, holistic disciplines. Honing her skills over the years, and redefining strategies through trial and error, she has been a trainer in school districts across Long Island and has presented at literacy workshops and conferences for federal and state-funded initiatives. Her philosophy and practice include educating and empowering her students to be self-sufficient learners. Faith works with all ages, preschoolers through adulthood, utilizing meta-cognitive strategies and multisensory instruction in a collaborative, non-threatening style, where parents are welcomed and encouraged to participate in the learning process.

Faith regularly blogs about literacy and learning on her website: http://highfiveliteracy.com. She provides professional development for teachers and school districts, as well as parent workshops, presentations, and private consultations.

In her free time, Faith enjoys spending time with her family, exercising, and ballroom dancing.

63808444R00075

Made in the USA
Middletown, DE
05 February 2018